A Guide To Unlimited
AUTISM SUCCESS

The proven blueprint for any dedicated
parent or carer that wants to help their
autistic child thrive in every area of
their development...despite unsupportive
schools, limited resources and without
spending a fortune on alternative therapies.

EMMA OTTAWAY

A Guide to Unlimited Autism Success

First published in Great Britain in 2016 by Compass Publishing

ISBN 978-1-907308-83-3

Set by The Book Refinery Ltd
Cover by Nehara (creativelog)

This publication is designed to provide accurate and authoritative information for Coaches, Trainers & Consultants. It is sold under the express understanding any decisions or actions you take as a result of reading this book must be based on your commercial judgement and will be at your sole risk. The author will not be held responsible for the consequences of any actions and/or decisions taken as a result of any information given or recommendations made.

Contents

Contents

Introduction

You're about to read some of the most successful tips and strategies for getting the best from your autistic child. You will be taken step by step through how to put these strategies in place so they work for you and more importantly your child. You'll discover insights about your child's complex needs and more, but...

There's a big but here...nothing you read about will work with your child if you don't.

You may feel that every day is a fight... with your child's school, with their doctors, their needs, with the local authorities and so on...

And let me tell you, it may well be that way.

I'm going to be honest with you...nobody will fight for your child more than you. And that's a hard pill to swallow. It's difficult, painful and can at times seem down right unfair.

But it's up to you to fight so that your child gets everything they deserve, or no one will.

My plan is that the help you receive in this book will make your fight a little easier.

Why this book?

This book has been designed to give you a clearer understanding of your autistic child's needs and how you can get the very best from them.

In this book you'll discover easy to follow proven strategies that will help you communicate better with your autistic child. You'll get simple tips and techniques to help you form that close, essential bond with your child and connect with them on an emotional level that may not have seemed possible before.

You'll learn how to support your child's unique sensory needs so that overall they feel in control of their bodies and can live with ease. You can also expect tried and tested techniques and recommended speech tools for your whole family to try out, in order to help support and encourage your child's language and form an emotional bond with their siblings.

My aim is to provide you with various proven strategies to help you ultimately support your child's development and set them up for success, enjoy!

A Special gift from *'The Ambitious Autism Ambassador'*

Before you go any further, make sure you go to www.unlimitedautismsuccess.com/book-resources and claim over £47 worth of additional tools and templates to help you get the very best from your child with autism.

Here's just some of what you'll get:

- Templates and ideas to help you better manage your child's behaviour

- Additional resources to help aid and improve your child's communication

- Helpful hints and tips to make sure your child is getting the support they need at school

- A ton of things you and the family can do to help your child progress socially and form bonds with others.

- And much more...

To get your FREE bonuses go to...
www.unlimitedautismsuccess.com/book-resources *now.*

SECTION ONE:

BEHAVIOUR

"Sometimes the only thing people see is what someone did. When in fact, they should be looking at why they did it."

~Unknown

Introduction to Behaviour

When it comes to your child's behaviour, you need to look a bit closer and realise that every single behaviour is your child's way of communicating. In some way or another, they are trying to tell you something through their behaviour.

When we look at a child's behaviour, ultimately we are assessing whether it is appropriate or inappropriate. Like most things, society decides what constitutes appropriate or inappropriate behaviour.

To give you an example;

It is okay or 'socially acceptable' to sing out loud while listening to the radio, with your car windows open, when you're in traffic. But it's not okay or 'socially acceptable' to sing out loud when you're on a train or bus.

This can be very confusing for an autistic child.

Autistic behaviour has and to this day continues to be researched and tested in great detail, in an effort to help us understand their way of thinking.

So going back to what we said earlier about how every behaviour is our child's way of communicating something to us, we also have to look at the inappropriate behaviours this way.

Firstly, let's be clear on what an inappropriate behaviour is. Inappropriate behaviour is when a child's home life, schooling or social situations are being sabotaged in some way. Often our natural reaction is to stop, block or extinguish these inappropriate behaviours, but I've found that with autistic children especially, this technique really isn't enough.

I say this because if your child's inappropriate behaviour is giving them sensory fulfilment in some way, then preventing them from engaging in this behaviour is not going to be effective. Because they are still going to be seeking that sensory feedback.

However, if you replace the behaviour with an appropriate substitute, i.e. One that gives them the same fulfilment, then you are well on your way to managing your child's challenging behaviours effectively.

Here are some examples of why an autistic child might engage in inappropriate behaviours in the first place:

- Sensory issues or overload

- Emotional overload

- Not knowing what is expected of them

- Not understanding what is expected of them

- Not remembering what is expected of them. (They may have known the rules to a game yesterday but struggle with them today.)

- Avoidance to an uncomfortable or unpleasant task

- Confusion over the way you communicate (e.g. unclear picture cards)

- Food sensitivities

- Physical pain

- Sleep deprivation

- Hunger or dehydration

All of these behaviours are a way of communicating. And it's up to us as their parent or carer to identify what our children are trying to say, then guide them to communicate their needs in an appropriate way.

Behaviour: Part One

Obsessive and repetitive behaviour is something you often see in children with autism. Unlike the majority of children who go through crazes, with one game being their favourite one week and something entirely different the next. Autistic children, on the other hand, can have one obsession they would do or talk about all day if they could! This type of obsessing can have an enormous impact on their behaviour and can become a real challenge if it's not dealt with in the right way. It can also affect their communication and learning.

I once worked with a child who was obsessed with public transport. He knew train lines by heart and had memorised entire bus timetables. It was all about numbers for this particular boy.. He was fascinated by the patterns he saw in the bus timetables and when riding on the buses, enjoyed being able to identify each approaching stop. Although this was a fantastic skill to have, it also had down sides....

For example;

If on any particular day a bus wasn't running to its usual schedule, this would develop into a highly stressful situation for him.

He wasn't able to understand that sometimes buses run late and don't arrive at the times stated on the timetable. His anxiety would then build up, until he couldn't control it and would go into meltdown.

A simple bus delay, something that a neuro-typical person would just shrug off as an irritation, can leave an autistic child feeling distressed for hours or even the rest of the day.

So what can you do about it?

Become their personal superhero and make sure there are never any complications in their life?

You may laugh at that comment, but I have met families that have tried to do this, and they have ended up fighting a losing battle.

Of course you can't plan for every little potential change to their environment.

BUT what you can do is:

1. Specifically identify what their obsession is.

AND

2. Find out their function to the obsession e.g., why they like a certain thing so much.

You will have a massive advantage when you do both these things, because now you can be in control of the obsession.

The first thing you can now do is to use their obsession as a reward or motivator for appropriate behaviour. The same way a reward chart or any other reward system works, something you know for sure that will really encourage your child to behave in the way you're asking.

Secondly, you can set boundaries for how long they can do or talk about their obsession and even make this part of their daily routine, so that it's clear and easy for them to understand. For example, the child who is obsessed with public transport could ask everyone in his family at dinner time about their journeys to work or school. Then once everyone has answered, the conversation is finished.

And finally, once you know the function, e.g., number patterns. You can encourage new games and activities with the same theme so that your child doesn't get stuck on one particular thing.

Behaviour: Part Two

I started out working with autistic children in schools all over London and during this period, I often had to deal with challenging behaviours, especially during play times. I'd be standing in a play area looking over a mass of children, who were racing around on bikes, jumping with skipping ropes and bouncing balls. My eyes and ears would be wide open, looking for any problems that might occur and trying my best to encourage social play. I learnt that play areas can be a very overwhelming place for a child with autism, and sometimes they'll show this through inappropriate behaviours.

One school I had worked at had a small and somewhat overcrowded playground and because of this, they had a large amount of incidents occurring with the children. The school recognised this and soon introduced ABC data recovery as part of their protocol when dealing with a playground incident.

For those of you that haven't come across an ABC data collection, it is a way of collecting and sharing accurate data regarding the behaviour of a child, with the aim of identifying the function and the triggers for the child's behaviour.

A typical ABC sheet has three columns to write information they are labelled A, B, and C.

A stands for Antecedent – What happened before the behaviour?

B stands for Behaviour – Description of the behaviour you saw/ heard.

C stands for Consequence - What did you do after the behaviour?

There is also an area to write the date, time, and location.

The idea is that when an incident occurs, you will immediately fill out an ABC sheet. Then with this precise data, you can track patterns that indicate the child's function and the triggers of the behaviour.

Triggers can be notoriously difficult to figure out if a child's behaviour is inconsistent. But ABC data is a clear way to compare behaviours on paper rather than just by memory.

By having a physical copy of the ABC's, I find it easier to find the trigger for the behaviour.

Once the function of the behaviour is identified, you can work out a replacement for that behaviour. For example, if the behaviour was biting and the child was sensory seeking, you could make sure that this child has access to chew sticks at all times. A bowl of crunchy cereal or a buttery corn on the cob, are good edible alternatives to chew sticks.

ABC data sheets are quick and easy to down load onto a computer or if you don't have one at the time, a notepad will also do just fine. (Later in this section I have created a template ABC data sheet for your use)

Make sure if you're keeping the ABC data at home, that your data sheets are somewhere that you can access them quickly, if you need to. If appropriate and your child is safe, start filling out your data once your child has engaged in the behaviour, while the ABC's are fresh in your mind, if you can't do this then wait until after you've given your child a consequence and then fill out the sheet.

Record as much detail as possible. Notes are fine. I find bullet points are the easiest and quickest way to list everything. Make sure your ABC's are dated before you store them in a file.

Behaviour: Part Three

When a child with autism has a meltdown, no matter where you are, it can be challenging to manage and an emotionally difficult thing to see. It's only natural for a parent or carer in this situation to feel overwhelmed and want to help their child feel better. Unfortunately if you don't fully understand your child's behaviour, you can end up doing the wrong thing entirely.

So...

Next time your child is having a meltdown, take a deep breath and try to remember these simple steps.

First things first, focus on changing the environment NOT your child. If you look close enough, the majority of the time, you'll find that the environment is in some way over-stimulating. And if like many autistic children, your child has 'Sensory Sensitivity', it is even more important to look at this. If your child can not tolerate bright lights or loud noise, for example, you may need to adjust the lighting in the room or move to a quieter area of the park. It's all about 'picking your battles' and if it's easy to make a few changes to prevent that meltdown, then my advice would always be to do this first.

Although it may not always be appropriate or possible to change the environment, this is when you'll need to look into alternative solutions. A few examples include wearing earplugs in a bowling alley so they can enjoy their favourite activities, or using a weighted snake/ vest to help them sit at the dining table for dinner.

Something that we often forget is NOT to try and 'talk your child round'. I assure you keeping your language clear and minimal will help you and your child a whole lot more. When a child with autism is in meltdown if, as we discussed before, it has been caused by overstimulation, then verbal communication will only exacerbate this and lead them to feel more frustrated. But this doesn't mean you can't communicate with them at all if you feel your child needs communication, keep your language short and sweet, or the use of flash cards is another option.

Always be clear and precise. As most autistic children are logical thinkers, you need to be clear with what you say to them to ensure you are giving off the right message. It's important that when the meltdown has finished, you tell your child what is 'safe' and appropriate behaviour and exactly what you expect from them. Of course tailor your language to your child's level of understanding. Research has shown children need boundaries and expectations, and guess what? Children with autism are no different. You can also do this by using visuals, if this works better for your child.

Think to yourself, is it a sensory need? Some autistic children crave sensory input throughout their daily life and this causes overstimulation and meltdowns. If you or someone else (therapist/ teacher) recognises this type of sensory need in your child, then it may just be a case of finding the right balance for your child. A way of achieving this balance can be through sensory toys, textured fabrics, music or deep pressure massage. I once worked with a child that took 'play putty' to the supermarket and he'd happily sit in his mother's trolley and play with his putty for the duration of the trip. It helped him stay calm and focused on one sensory need, whilst still getting sensory feedback.

If possible distract and diverse. Sometimes the simplest distraction can work wonders, but as we know, when you're involved in a highly stressful meltdown situation, the simple answers don't always pop into your head. A few examples of distractions include a squeeze ball, a calming sensory toy or listening to some calming music. It goes without saying that they should be away from others to create a safe and calming atmosphere, in which case that may be enough to calm the majority of the frustration. Every child is different.

When you have a minute to yourself, try to figure out the trigger. Note the kind of environment your child was in at the time of the meltdown, this will help you figure out what the cause was or help detect a function or pattern. Think about the time of day, the clothing they were wearing, smells and noises - anything that was going on around them at the time. Look at yourself or others around them, at the time were you expecting too much from your child? Once you've discovered exactly what it was that triggered the meltdown, then you can tackle it..

Although it's tough, you need to remain calm. Seeing your child have a meltdown is undoubtedly a frustrating and upsetting experience for you, especially if it happens in a public area. Your child is already over stimulated and seeing you in highly emotional state will only add to that overstimulation. Once you have created an environment in which they are in safe, take a breather. Stay calm and focus your attention on figuring out the reason for the behaviour to help prevent more meltdowns in the future.

Behaviour: Part Four

Sleep issues are very common in children with autism.

So first things first, if you're reading this and you have a child with sleep problems, you are not alone. Although, it might feel that way when you're up at 3am with your child on a Monday morning.

Believe me, you won't be the only one.

Whether your child struggles to fall asleep at night or wakes up excessively early, this is an issue that often affects the whole family and needs to be addressed.

Therapists recommend that before bed you should engage in calming activities with your child. Not only to help them relax but to let them know it's 'winding down time' and they will soon be going to bed. TV and video games are not recommended in this hour of wind down time, as it can arouse them and have the opposite affect. However, calming music, bubble baths and massage are great ways to help your child relax.

Once you've decided to commit to improving your child's sleep routine, you need to follow a simple strategy to extinguish their current behaviours and then stick with it. Below are *three tips for the most common sleep issues I've come across in children with autism.*

Tip one: If your child doesn't like to be left at night or they're moving into a new bed/ bedroom, it's essential that when it's their bed time, you leave the room.

This is probably my number one tip regarding sleep problems, if this instruction is not followed it can cause challenging sleep attachment issues for you in the future, so it's best for you to avoid this in the early stages.

Tip two: If there is no problem when your child goes to bed, but find they get up continually during the night then you need to be strict with yourself. Explain to them before bed that they need to stay in their room, if appropriate give them an incentive to stay there, e.g., you will make their favourite breakfast in the morning or read their favourite book to them if they do. Then if you find them out of their bedroom during the night, silently take them back, giving them minimal attention. The 'minimal attention' part is paramount here. This action may need to be repeated several times, but be strong and keep with it.

Tip three: This one is for the parents who have an early riser! The children that wake up at what I call, 'silly AM' and they're determined that everyone else in the house wakes up with them. If this sounds like your family, then you're also in for some hard work. Follow the same instructions as tip two above, but explain to your child before bed that they need to stay in their room in the morning until you come in and get them. Ensure that each time you need to take them back to their room in the morning you give as little attention as possible. This technique shows that you are not rewarding them for their inappropriate behaviour.

Behaviour: Part Five

Ever asked your child a question 10 times and they just refuse? You word the question in four or five different ways but they just aren't having it?

You've had it...

You're exhausted...

Drained...

Out of ideas...

And all you wanted to do was dress your child in a t-shirt because it's 33 degrees outside.

I once worked with a boy whose mother had just had her second child. Matthew's parents were worried about how he would react to the new baby even before he'd been born. You see, Matthew hated loud noises and they were worried about how he would react to a crying baby.

The baby was about 10 days old when Matthew went to school very unhappy.

Matthew jumped off the school bus....

Ran into the school....

Sprinted down the corridor and into the classroom.

I was already in the classroom at the time so his entrance shocked me.

"Wahhhh wahhhhhh wahhhhhhh." Matthew shouted repeatedly as he paced up and down the carpeted area.

We usually took the children straight to the toilet once they arrived, but I knew I'd have to pick my battles that morning.

I waited 30 seconds to see if Matthew had calmed down by himself. Then I went into one of our sensory toy boxes and took out one of his favourite toys. I sat next to him and turned the ball upside down. The tiny balls that were inside the ball made a calm swishing sound as they fell to the bottom.

Matthew recognised the sound he fell silent and turned around to look at the ball.

"Hey Matthew, that's a nice quiet voice, shall we play with the ball together?" I asked him quietly.

Matthew thought about it for a few seconds then...

"Wahhhhhhh wahhhhhhh wahhhhhhhhhh" continued and he was once again shouting and pacing around the room.

The other children were due any second. I had to make sure he was calm before they arrived or this would turn into a difficult morning, but...

Too late!

Sammy, Alfie and Katie were there at the door with their teaching assistant.

"Hey, can we come in!" She sang out happily to me. I opened the door. Jo, the assistant, ignored Matthew and took the other children through to the toilets.

After observing the other children, Matthew was now jumping up and down on the spot shouting louder, "Wahhhhhhh wahhhhh wahhhhhhhh!"

I could hear the children finishing up in the bathroom and I could also hear Sammy saying, "shhhhhh shhhhhhhh shhhhhh!"

I looked at Matthew.

Another member of staff, who was helping us for the morning, walked in at that moment.

"Matthew, let's go to the nature garden." I said and calmly took his hand.

I asked the assistant to continue on with the normal morning routine, and assured her that we'd be back soon.

She nodded happily.

I walked slowly with Matthew to the nature garden. He was silent the whole way, so I praised him on his calm behaviour and quiet walking.

We got to the nature garden and I let go of his hand, then....Like a jack-in-the-box, he sprung to life again....

"Wahhhhhhh wahhhhhhh wahhhhhhh" he screamed.

Damn! I thought he'd calmed down!

I reached for the small noisy ball which I'd grabbed and tucked into my pocket on the way out of the classroom. Matthew watched silently as it lit up and listened as it made space like noises.

"I like the space sounds, let's listen again." I told him. Silently he watched and listened. I pressed the ball again.

"Sit with me Matthew and let's listen to the ball again." I said. Staring at me the whole time, Matthew sat down next to me.

"I love how quiet it is!" I told him, smiling. He reached for the ball. I held it out to him, holding onto it.

"Want space ball." Matthew asked in a calm voice.

YESSSSSS! I thought.

"Great asking Matthew, here go you." I said. I let him play with the ball for two minutes he played beautifully with no shouting at all.

I told him, "One more minute with the space ball Matthew."

I waited until his breathing had returned to normal then said: "It's circle time, let's go back to rabbit class."

He stood up silently and obediently and we walked back together to the classroom.

That was one of the first times I used a declarative with a challenging child.

A declarative is the opposite of a question when used in a sentence.

For example with Matthew I said: "Let's go to the nature garden." Instead of, "Do you want to go to the nature garden?"

Some other great examples are:

> *"I'm so hot in my jumper." Instead of, "Aren't you hot in your jumper?"*

> *"Here is some apple to eat." Instead of, "Do you want some apple to eat?"*

> *"Let's walk to school." Instead of, "Shall we walk to school today?"*

Declarative sentences can work really well when you're in a challenging situation with your child.

The statement can be enough to throw your child off track and listen.

Try out some declaratives at home and let me know how you get along.

Behaviour Q&A's

"My son is on the spectrum and he is 7 years old. We are currently facing some challenging behaviours from him. Our son has never really tolerated hand holding or being carried by us. He often wanders away from our house but recently this "running away" type behaviour is becoming more frequent. How can I stop him from running off like this? I'm so worried."

This behaviour is called "Elopement" and can be very difficult to deal with for the parents and carers of autistic children, As well as preventing this behaviour from happening, you also need to look at some safety measures, that you can take. If your child is wandering away, look at how you can modify your home to make it safer. Some ways of doing this are by installing security cameras in your home, having secure locks fitted to all doors and a house alarm. You may also want to consider motion detectors or alarms on your main doors. Make sure you exchange all contact info with at least a few of your neighbours and if you feel comfortable, tell them that your son sometimes wanders away from home so they can be aware of the situation. The more people that know about your son's situation, the safer he will be if he wanders off into your community.

Once all your safety measures are in place, sit down and try to determine the trigger for his eloping behaviour. For example, look into whether there is a pattern, perhaps a certain time of day when the behaviour occurs most. Many children with autism will see something they find interesting and try to go after it without realising the consequences of their behaviour. Once you've discovered the trigger or triggers for your child's behaviour, you can then find replacement behaviours to teach and for your child to engage in. Explain these alternatives to your child, or if necessary make an 'outdoors' picture card and teach that they can ask for this and someone will go with them.

Make it clear that at night the 'outdoors' card is put away as going outdoors at night is not allowed.

"My son who is two and a half is non-verbal. He is lashing out a lot and biting both children and adults. How can I control this?"

It is important that violent or aggressive behaviours are dealt with immediately. If you have a behaviour consultant or analyst on board working with your child, they can conduct an assessment to determine the cause of their biting behaviour. If not, I would advise you to collect ABC data when these situations happen. ABC's data collection is an easy and effective way of identifying the function and trigger of a child's behaviour. If your child is also biting at school, ask the teachers to fill out some ABC sheets, which may help in determining any triggers and this way you may have clearer details each time this behaviour occurs. Below Is a typical ABC chart I've put together.

(See part 2, page 13 of this section for a detailed description of how to use ABC data and the purpose for it.)

Date, Time & Location	Antecedent What happened before the behaviour?	Behaviour Describe the behaviour. Everything you saw/ heard	Consequence What did you do after the behaviour?

When dealing with a child that bites and the function or trigger is unknown, you need to be mindful that they could bite at any given time. Avoid placing parts of your body close to their mouth and make sure you can see your child at all times especially when they are with other people, just until this behaviour is under control.

"I have two children, my 4-year-old son who has autism and my daughter who is almost 2 years old and neuro-typical. My daughter often reaches out to my son to play with him but he ignores her. If she comes too close to him while he is playing, he will either walk away, and play somewhere else, or physically push her away from him. What can I do to help them bond and play together as brother and sister?"

Often social skills do not come naturally to children with autism, therefore, they need to be taught. The behaviour your son is showing towards his sister is probably all that he knows. But once you teach him how to play appropriately he will learn other ways to interact with her.

As many times as you can fit in a week, do an activity that involves both of your children. At first, something less demanding of your son to ease him into the idea of having his sister around, colouring or painting together is a good example. Sit with them and model appropriate social behaviour. Reinforce good sitting together, sharing, eye contact and gentle hands. Over-exaggerate the positive reinforcement, really show your son how happy you are when he shows appropriate social behaviours.

If your son responds well to visuals, create or invest in a star chart so he can receive colourful star stickers each time he displays the appropriate behaviours. Begin by giving him a star for simply tolerating sitting with his sister. Show him you're happy with this and he will be more likely to sit with her again, to receive more stars.

This modelling will need to be repeated often. But over time by following this strategy, your child will begin to learn how to play appropriately with his sister.

"My son is 7, he was diagnosed with Autism at the age of 3. He has always been inflexible in his thinking and finds change hard to accept. At school he gets very upset when his day is 'different' he cries and lies on the floor refusing to move. We also get this at home. How can I prepare him or help him deal with changes?"

Rigid thinking and difficulty accepting change are common traits that children with autism display. It's likely this stems from their security in the predictability of life. But when this is taken away, our children feel a lack of understanding and control, and this upsets them.

A few quick tips for you to help your child accept change are by what I call 'semi alerting them' about change. For example, if you're at home or school you can use either a written or picture schedule. Write the new activity in a green pen or if using a picture draw a green circle around it. This way the new activity won't come as a total surprise to them. When your son is at school, encourage his teachers to engage in small changes throughout the day, for example walk down a different staircase when going for lunch. Small exposures to change will help your son accept changes better when it inevitably arrives.

Do the same at home, make changes fun not scary. Explain that you're not having spaghetti for dinner, like you had previously told him, but instead you're making his favourite meal. If it's appropriate and reinforcing for him, let him help you cook, really get him involved.

A Special gift from *'The Ambitious Autism Ambassador'*

Before you go any further, make sure you go to www.unlimitedautismsuccess.com/book-resources and claim over £47 worth of additional tools and templates to help you get the very best from your child with autism.

Here's just some of what you'll get:

- Templates and ideas to help you better manage your child's behaviour

- Additional resources to help aid and improve your child's communication

- Helpful hints and tips to make sure your child is getting the support they need at school

- A ton of things you and the family can do to help your child progress socially and form bonds with others.

- And much more...

To get your FREE bonuses go to...
www.unlimitedautismsuccess.com/book-resources *now.*

SECTION TWO:

COMMUNICATION

"To effectively communicate, we must realise that we are all different in the way we perceive the world and use this understanding as a guide to our communication with others."

~ Anthony Robbins

Introduction to Communication

Most children with autism have to overcome many challenges to be able to communicate appropriately with us. While a typical developing child can easily communicate through facial expressions, gestures, eye contact and spoken language, children with autism can really struggle to express themselves in these ways. This is due to their visual processing, their over or under sensitive systems and fundamentally their impaired social thinking.

After all...if a child does not think 'socially' why would they act socially?

A lot of the time we cannot (and should not) predict what children with autism are thinking, due to their lack of these communicative skills. It's up to us to look for the tiny clues our children give that shows what they are interested in and also their desire to communicate with us.

And I can assure you of one thing...

When you become a conscious listener, you will suddenly see all of the attempts your autistic child shows to communicate. Then with this precious new knowledge, you can respond to your child and begin to build new, clearer ways for them to communicate and for you to finally teach them new ways of communication.

Research has shown that:

"55% of communication is body language, 38% is tone of voice and 7% is the actual spoken words."

7% spoken words!

Yet language is one of the most essential milestones we wait for in our developing children. And when our children grow into adulthood, speech is still valued more highly than body language or tone of voice.

In my years working in special needs schools across the UK, the phrase that was repeated throughout each school over and over again was, *"Use your words."* And because of this obsessive focus on language, the small non-verbal attempts that our autistic children make to communicate with us are often missed.

That's a sad reality for many parents and carers of children with autism.

But...what I'm saying to you is that is doesn't have to be *YOUR* reality.

Once you observe your child's behaviours, pick up on their communication attempts and respond to their wants and needs.

Keep a diary and note down when your child attempts to communicate with you. Once you've recognised the type of behaviour they usually show, you can go about teaching them more appropriate ways. Such as tapping your arm, approaching you or bringing a game over to you that they want to play.

Communication: Part One

As communication can be very daunting for many children with autism, it's important that we as parents and careers handle the subject with care and understanding. For many autistic children, regardless of age, being asked or expected to spontaneously begin a conversation can be a terrifying and highly stressful task.

When taking part in any activity, all children need a clear expectation from the adult in charge. For example, if you're taking your child to the park, the expectation may be that your child plays where you can see them and comes when you call them. This expectation would commonly be told to the child before they enter the park. And believe it or not, our literal thinking ASD children are no different! So if you want to work on your child's communication skills, you'll need to follow the same instructions, think of it as a recipe.

In order for an autistic child to initiate a conversation, you'll need to give them some pointers:

Firstly - narrow it down for your child. Give them a starting point, a subject to talk about. Just doing this alone can lift a huge amount of pressure off them. If you think about the endless topics of conversation they have to choose from and then to find the relevant information to use, this, would be very daunting and probably stressful for them. Personally, I'm a very chatty person who loves meeting new people and communicating, but I can see why such a task could be stressful for a child with autism. So simply giving them a topic to talk about, can help them focus.

Secondly - give your child a time scale for how long the conversation will last. As autistic children are usually visual thinkers, a sand timer or stopwatch may work well for this. By giving them a time limit to talk, you're giving them a clear expectation that will hopefully minimise their anxiety. Two minutes has shown to be the most appropriate starting point for autistic children to talk on a topic, so use this as a guide. To help eliminate any remaining anxiety you could tell your child beforehand that they can have two minutes to collect their thoughts, and then your two minute conversation can commence.

If your child trails off the subject, just remind them of the conversation subject in a calm manner and then continue. This is not a problem.

Try repeating the two minute conversations daily to get the best results. Research has shown that meal times are an ideal opportunity to practice family socialising and communication, so why not try out this strategy then. Also to ensure that your child doesn't lose interest in these two minute conversations, change the subjects daily. To make it fun, have a jar on the table and fill it with conversation topics written on small cards, and let your child do a 'lucky dip' to choose their topic!

Communication: Part Two

There's one little 'w' word that we use so often in life, and we expect to get answers straight after. No one is at fault here, we all do this with our autistic children, myself included. It's a natural word to come out of our mouths and sometimes we don't even realise that we've used it. We sometimes ask it out of anger, frustration, curiosity or even to be reassured.

The word I'm talking about is, *"why"*

Can you hear yourself saying it now?

Behaviour experts that specialise in autism, say that the majority of ASD children do not know or totally understand why they've behaved in a certain way.

For example, your child may have lashed out at his sister because he can no longer stand the overwhelming smell of her nappy! But he doesn't know how to tell you that.

Or...

He might hate the tightness of the trousers you dressed him in that day and he couldn't stand the uncomfortable feeling any longer, so he stripped off in the coffee shop.

But because your child can't express these reasons to you, they behave inappropriately, by lashing out or taking off their clothes. And, these situations naturally alert us to use the dreaded 'w' word....*"**Why** did you do that?"*

Like I said it feels natural for us to ask why, so if you're reading this and you've realised that you ask your autistic child 'why', please don't feel bad. Raising and working with autistic children is all about learning. And now you know this, you can be open to change.

Asking your child with autism why they've behaved in a certain way could only put unnecessary pressure on them, which is likely to make their behaviour escalate quicker.

If you're reading this and thinking, *"What should I say instead?"* Here are some examples to help you out:

- *"What do you need to do now?"*

- *"What did you just do?"*

- *"Was that a good/ bad choice that you just made?"*

- *"What could you have done instead?"*

- *"What can we do now to make sure that doesn't happen again?"*

Communication: Part Three

When communicating with autistic children you need to keep in the forefront of your mind that ASD children are literal and very precise in the way that they think. I've come to realise that children with autism speak very specifically about things, which makes a lot of sense!

The thing is...

We often speak *sloppily*.

Like it or not, we do!

Think about it...if you were somewhere with a loved one and you wanted a photo taken, it's likely you'd find someone and say, "Can you take a picture please?"

And the majority of the time, the people that you'd ask would understand this sloppy talk. Their minds would tell them, 'they want me to take a photo of them' rather than just 'a picture' like what was asked of them. So because the vast majority understand us, why would we think to change our language?

But if you make an effort to use specific language when you speak to your autistic child, I assure you that together you will communicate more effectively, and you'll notice a change in the way your child responds to your new 'literal' communication.

Try out this technique whilst doing a relaxing activity like reading with your child. Let's say your child's favourite book is "Rainbow Fish" a childhood classic, and you're reading the book together. Your child is looking at the beautiful shiny pictures and he points at the rainbow fish.

You may have said "Fish!" As you pointed, but this time you would speak more clearly and say "This is a Rainbow fish, he is colourful!"

Or another example of using careful, specific language in the natural environment, is if your child reaches out for your hot mug of coffee.

You may automatically say "No, don't touch!" A more effective response would be "Don't touch the mug because it's hot and you could hurt yourself." This way you're explaining in a detailed and clearer way what you want your child to do.

So just by adding a few tweaks to your language and by being consistent with this strategy, your child is much more likely to understand and respond to you in a more appropriate way.

If you feel that your child will struggle to take in and understand the increase in language, try using shorter sentences but keep to the important specific language. For example, "Rainbow fish is colourful" or, "Don't touch, the mug's hot and it will hurt."

Communication: Part Four

Children with Autism don't always show us what they want in the same way neuro-typical children would. For example, I once worked with a parent whose son would (what felt like) constantly follow her around saying the same phrases.

"Shoes on."

"MacDonalds on Friday."

"Turn TV off."

She told me about his behaviour and asked my advice as to what she should say to him. I explained to her that I didn't think her son wanted a specific response to his recurring phrases. This was just his way of showing his mum that he was desperate to communicate with her and that's all he knew.

The mother gave me a bewildered look.

Then I explained it to her like this...

If you were going on a trip to France, you would know beforehand there would probably be points in your trip where you would need to attempt to speak a little french. But if you're anything like me then you don't have a vast vocabulary bank of French phrases. Mine pretty much consists of "Bonjour, Au revoir, Oui, Non, Merci" and a few randomly selected poorly pronounced adjectives remembered from school. So it's safe to say that when I communicate with French people it doesn't run smoothly.

I remember being 12 years old and going on my first overnight school trip to Calais.

The second we stopped, we all unbuckled our seat belts and raced off the coach, long before we were instructed to by our teachers.

....after all we were all so high on sugar from the sweets we'd been stuffing our faces with on the coach, we were pretty much unable to listen at this point.

Our teacher blew a whistle and forced us into a huddle and began explaining the plan for the day. I zoned out at the point where she began the 'health and safety' jargon and started to take in my surroundings.

I only took notice again when a friend nudged me, "You're with us" she said. I quickly realised we'd be in groups of four for the day and each group would have an adult with them.

I watched as a parent helper came toward us smiling. Then I heard my teacher say

"Your adult will now walk you towards the markets where you will be buying your lunch and ordering ...IN FRENCH! Good Luck!"

WHAT?! In French!

Are they being serious? I had only just learnt to say "Je m'appelle Emma." Badly.

By the time we reached the markets, I didn't care what I ate I just wanted some kind of food in my hands.

My friend went first, confidently she ordered her toasted baguette.

I was next.

Terrified, I looked up at the man on the stall...

"Err... toasted cheese sandwich, err... hot chocolate....as well... errrr... merci."

Stood bewildered, the man stared at me.

"Pain?" He said.

I could feel my "adults'" eyes staring at me, no doubt she'd have to give my teacher feedback on how we did when ordering our lunch. I was going to fail! But I was doing the best I could...I took a deep breath.

"Pain....yes...errr oui....et cheese....errr hot chocolate as well... errr... please merci."

There were many hand gestures involved here. But nope, the man wasn't getting it. He looked behind me at my "adult" for help. She jumped in and saved the day, ordering my lunch in fluent French..

I was a so relieved but embarrassed to say the least.

I had done the best I could.

But what I continued to do was use the same phrases and words over and over again, because that was all I knew, hoping that I'd be understood,.

Sound familiar?

Autistic children with limited language are doing just this. Using the same phrases and words and hoping to be understood.

As their parents and carers, we need to acknowledge this and be patient with them. Make suggestions, give them visuals to help them communicate appropriately and give verbal prompts to help them formulate their sentences. Regardless of how frustrating it may be for us, I guarantee you it is more frustrating for them.

Communication: Part Five

For children with Autism, initiating social interaction with other children can be challenging. I once observed a 5-year-old girl with ASD in the school playground, Becky's teachers wanted her observed so that they could formulate a strategy to help her socialise. They told me Becky would go over and watch her peers play every day, but if they noticed her watching and spoke to her, she would walk away and play by herself. Her teachers desperately wanted to help her make friends and play in a group and tried to help, but every time she'd just walk away.

So, sitting on a miniature plastic chair in the playground, I watched Becky. Within a few minutes, she ran outside in search of a playmate. She looked around for a while and then she spotted her friends. There were three girls playing with a large skipping rope in the corner of the playground. As predicted, Becky watched them without showing any interest in wanting to play. I curiously observed as the three girls continued to play, ignoring her completely.

It took all my strength not to get involved. All I wanted to do was help her out. But I trusted my gut and carried on watching the girls intently.

A minute or so passed, Becky was still hypnotised by the three girls. Then all of a sudden one of the girls put down her side of the skipping rope and walked towards Becky.

Becky stared at the girl wide-eyed.

"Do you wanna do ski....?" But before she could finish her invite, Becky had disappeared.

She literally ran away as soon as the girl was within four feet of her.

It was heart breaking to watch.

Looking both confused and disappointed, the little girl went back to join her friends. I looked around the playground for Becky and saw that she was walking along a low rise wall on the other side of the playground. She played by herself for five minutes before two boys playing caught her eye. This time, the two boys were chasing each other on small bikes. Becky was smiling this time as she watched them. The boys were far too excited in their game of chase to notice her. A few more minutes passed and then play time was over.

I thanked the teachers, gathered my things together, and made my way to my favourite coffee shop (where I do all my best thinking) to read over my notes and to write up a report...

I quickly made the connection between both the activities. Becky had watched the physical activities, and then when she played alone, she engaged herself in balancing on a beam. This demonstrated to me that Becky enjoyed physical play and possibly needed more of this in her daily routine. Her eye contact remained strong when she watched the children playing, there was a definite hypnotic look I'm her eyes. But as soon as any of the children showed an interest in Becky, her eye contact was broken and she ran away.

Becky was clearly missing vital social skills which would enable her to actually show her interest, in wanting to play with others.

I gulped down my latte, typed up my report and headed home.

Five weeks after I sent the report I was heading back to the school for a meeting about Becky. After my recommendations Becky had spent three weeks attending a social skills group run by the SENCO at school, she'd been given social cue cards to help her initiate conversation with her peers and I was told she'd grown in confidence in her class.

I was excited to see her, to say the least, I pretty much ran into the school...

Her SENCO met me in the reception. I had coincidently arrived just at break time, so she asked if I'd like to observe Becky.

Try and stop me!!! I nodded professionally and walked into the familiar playground.

Becky was sitting at a yellow table with two other girls taking part in a tea party. She was looking over at her friend and laughing hysterically at her while she ate her imaginary cupcake.

It was amazing to see such a huge change in Becky and what was equally amazing was to see such a great school determined to help one of their pupils. With just a few small changes Becky was able to socialise in the way she wanted too.

Sometimes parents and carers of children with autism can over think a problem, until it feels like they have a mountain to climb. But the solution can be simple if you take a few steps back. Getting other professionals on board to look at the problem with fresh eyes can be all you need.

Communication Q&A's

"My son is autistic and has been attending a special school for 4 years now, he enjoys school and is happy to go each morning. A year ago the school introduced PEC's and my son picked it up very quickly. He uses some language when he communicates but he is so reliant on his PEC's folder we have found it so hard to fade it away. What would you advise to help us?"

PEC's can be a great resource to kick start communication and it's fantastic that your son picked it up so quickly and that he is also using language. Although PEC's can be brilliant to use when communicating with ASD children, as with any type of prompting it's essential that you fade back the visuals as soon as possible. This is to make sure your child doesn't become lazy and uninterested in using their language. PEC's can sometimes have this effect on children with autism, so it's important that you keep the ball rolling. And not just that, let's face it, a big bulky folder full of laminated visuals can be somewhat impractical when you're out and about.

Depending on which stage your son is at with PEC's, you need to build on his language through extending the sentences used on the PEC's strip, i.e."I can see a brown bird outside, or I want a bowl of grapes and a drink please." Speaking the sentence as well as constructing and giving it to the desired person, is VITAL.

I also highly recommend a programme called *'Proloquo2go'* it's a great language tool for children with autism and I've seen many children develop their language from it alone. Check it out on Google as this may be a good alternative to PEC's and help to form fluent and natural language.

"My grandson is 4 years old and when I take him to eat out in public, he talks very loud. He also laughs loudly and makes loud squealing noises. How can I get him to be quieter when we are out?"

First, you need to teach your grandson to use an inside voice and an outside voice. A fun way of doing this is by taking him outside in your garden or a local park and demonstrating a loud 'outside voice' by shouting as loud as you can. Get him to join in of course! Then take him inside and demonstrate a quiet 'inside voice' for this use an exaggerated quiet voice so that there is a very clear difference between the two. Before you get to the restaurant, remind him that he needs to talk quietly and use his inside voice while you're there. Take fiddle toys if necessary to help him relax while this rule is being taught, and by all means continue to take them if you find he is sitting well and is quiet with them.

In the beginning it may be reinforcing to take a favourite toy e.g. an iPad and tell him if he sits nicely and uses his inside voice for two or three minutes (whatever time you feel is appropriate for him) then he can have the iPad for one minute, don't forget to take a visual timer. Then slowly increase the time he needs to be quiet, until eventually he is only getting the iPad at the end of your meal. Perhaps have it in the car or for the journey home.

"I have a daughter who is 4 and she has ASD. She is a very happy social little girl she loves playing with me. I recently cut down my working hours so I now have a lot more time at home with her. This is great, but I want to make sure my time with her is productive as at the moment she is happy to play but doesn't use any language at all. How can I encourage her to speak while we play?"

It's great that your daughter is keen to play with you. At the moment, it seems like she isn't using her language when you play because she doesn't feel like she needs to. Try out some new games where language is paramount for the game to work.

Outdoor play is a great way of promoting and learning a new language. And research has shown that physical movement gives children the sensory feedback they need which then promotes natural speech flow. Using play equipment like seesaws, swings and climbing frames are ideal for learning basic language concepts. Teach your daughter their labels and then the concepts such as, up/ down, in/out etc.

Children with autism enjoy repetition so play to her interests:

- Practice repetitive phrases in play, such as:

- On your marks, get set, go!

- 1, 2, 3!

- Ready, steady, go!

- Stop randomly while engaging in a fun activity and prompt her to ask for "more" repeat this with the things she is most enjoying.

- Blow bubbles and makes funny noises each time they pop. Then prompt "your turn" and model a sound as necessary.

Make sure whatever you're doing is fun for your daughter, if you feel something is too challenging for her, then tone it down. This shouldn't be hard work, if she's having fun, she is much more likely to begin using her language.

"I'm a preschool teacher and I have a boy with autism in my class. When I work one to one with him he speaks to me, but in a group or whole class environment he is mute. How can I get him to communicate with the children in his class?"

Communicating in a large group environment can be very daunting for many people. So it's understandable that children with autism, who may not be confident with speaking, can find communicating in a group highly stressful. But saying this, preschool 'snack time' can be a fantastic time to teach communication skills. Generally, children are highly motivated by food and making their wishes known during snack time will be important to them. So play on this, make snack time just as much about communication as it is eating a healthy snack. Two skills to begin by teaching are:

1. Getting a peers attention.

e.g. By tapping them on the shoulder, saying their name or giving them eye contact

2. Requesting an item of food or drink.

e.g. Pointing and asking, "Grapes please" Or if the child is more able, asking, "Can I have the grapes please, Jenny."

Each day, assign a child the job of 'snack time helper' to offer out snacks. Model the correct steps yourself first so they know to only respond to the appropriate request. This builds the motivation in each child to communicate correctly and if the child with autism sees his peers doing this and receiving their desired snack he will soon make the link and with encouragement, do so himself.

A Special gift from *'The Ambitious Autism Ambassador'*

Before you go any further, make sure you go to www.unlimitedautismsuccess.com/book-resources and claim over £47 worth of additional tools and templates to help you get the very best from your child with autism.

Here's just some of what you'll get:

- Templates and ideas to help you better manage your child's behaviour

- Additional resources to help aid and improve your child's communication

- Helpful hints and tips to make sure your child is getting the support they need at school

- A ton of things you and the family can do to help your child progress socially and form bonds with others.

- And much more...

To get your FREE bonuses go to...
www.unlimitedautismsuccess.com/book-resources *now.*

SECTION THREE:

SENSORY
INTEGRATION

"Even for parents of children that are not on the spectrum, there is no such thing as a normal child."

~ *Violet Stevens*

Introduction to Sensory Integration

When it comes to Autism, sensory integration is a topic that we can over think till it drives us crazy! Because, like everything, each child's sensory processing is totally unique to them.

Neuro-typical people have a vast amount of sensory abilities, most of which come so easy to us that we don't even need to think when to use them. But these abilities can be profoundly difficult for our children with autism to develop.

For example, walking flat-footed in a straight line can seem like a mountain to climb for an autistic child.

Many children with autism, struggle to identify where their body is and how to get to move in the way they want it to. And if a child is unaware of 'where their body is' this effects so much of their movement.

Here are a few things you need to know when learning about sensory integration:

- Sensory integration is the way we accept, take in and then organise sensations we receive internally and externally.

- This sensory input then travels through our neural system and into the brain. Once it reaches the brain, it is processed and finally, we respond to the input.

- Sight, smell, taste, hearing and touch are the most commonly known sensory systems but in actual fact, they are just five of the twenty one sensory systems we have operating inside of us.

- A child with autism receives a cocktail of atypical signals along with lost and crossed connections in the journey between their sensory system and their brain. And the result is that children with autism deal with some immensely challenging experiences related to their senses.

- Autistic children struggle with their sensory systems being overwhelmed AND underwhelmed by their environment. We call this hyperacute and hypoacute.

In '1001 Great Ideas For Teaching & Raising Children With Autism or Aspergers', Ellen Notbohm and Veronica Zysk explain that;

"Sensory integration dysfunction is at the root of many of the core difficulties of autism spectrum disorders. It affects behaviour, communication, nutrition and sleep-critical functions that dictate the quality of the environment your child must live in, minute to minute day to day, year to year."

So this section is all about identifying the sensory struggles your child has and learning some simple techniques to help them deal with this effectively.

Sensory Integration: Part One

Many years ago, I worked with a little boy who really struggled to cope with his sensory needs, and as a result he found many everyday tasks a real struggle.

At school, Luke was eager to learn, but he had a huge barrier holding him back and this really upset him. He engaged in repetitive physical and verbal 'stimming' which ended up isolating him from his classmates and limiting the learning he could access.

Luke was observed numerous times, by different professionals who asked questions, took notes, changed things, brought in new programmes but nothing seemed to really work for the long term.

Luke's teachers didn't know what to do.

Luke's parents were out of ideas.

And Luke began to regress and soon resisted going to school.

One of the tasks Luke found particularly difficult was walking down the corridor to his classroom at the start of the day. He lost his balance so frequently that in the end he gave up and reverted to crawling.

One morning Luke had dropped to the floor and I was doing my best to encourage him to stand up and guide him to the classroom. A colleague who was to the left of me, was on standby to help out if necessary. While we were in the corridor I noticed something, there was a lady watching us, I didn't recognise her but she was smiling. What with being caught up with Luke and not having a clue who she was, I ignored her and carried on with what I was doing.

Later that day there was a knock at the door...the same face I had seen that morning was there at our door, smiling at us again. Anyway, she introduced herself as Chloe the new OT (Occupational Therapist) and then explained that she would be working with Luke and that she'd seen us this morning in the corridor. She went on to ask all the same questions that the other professionals who had previously met Luke had done, she then took Luke's hand and led him out for their session.

At the end of the day, Chloe came into our classroom once again and explained Luke's sensory needs to us in more detail.

Once again, we listened.

She said she would be using a 'weighted rucksack' to help Luke walk independently to the classroom in the mornings and she'd be starting from tomorrow.

We were all pretty overwhelmed with Chloe's 'get up and go' attitude and personally I couldn't wait to see what the next day would bring.

Tomorrow came and Chloe greeted Luke at the door with his new rucksack, she put it on his back, steadied him slightly and told him to walk to the Green class.

We all watched and silently spurred him on.

And to our amazement, for the first time he walked down, slowly and a little wobbly but, he did it!

And for the rest of the academic year Luke walked with his rucksack happily and made great progress in many other areas.

Sensory integration dysfunction can be an extremely big challenge for our autistic children and for us to deal with. But with the right professionals on board your child can achieve their sensory goals. There are many other 'Chloe's' out there with fresh new ideas for our ASD children, so don't give up when you feel that a challenge is too big for your child.

You may also want to think about finding a private OT for your child so they have more hours of therapy. Or perhaps approach the school's Special Needs Coordinator for advice on meeting the sensory needs of your child. They may be able to recommend some useful resources.

Sensory Integration: Part Two

Children with Autism will experience the classic five senses (sight, sound, taste, touch & hearing) in an entirely different way to which typically developing children do. And because of this fact, it's important that parents and carers monitor the activities we set up for autistic children.

Why?

Well there's thousands of reasons why. To ensure you aren't setting your child up to fail if the activity is too challenging. To ensure it's reinforcing so that you get the best out of your child. To have fun! All children are more likely to interact whilst they're enjoying themselves. And importantly to ensure the activity isn't going to promote a 'Sensory Overload' for your child.

Now, let me explain exactly what a sensory overload is:

A sensory overload is when a person's sensory system is *over-stimulated* as a result of their over or under sensory system in the current environment.

When autistic children experience this, they cannot cope with their overwhelming feelings and they can get extremely upset as a result.

All children react differently when they have sensory overload.

I've seen children experience a sensory overload many times when they engage in their favourite sensory activity over and over again. Even though it's something they enjoy, whether it's messy or just sensory play for example.

Ever heard of the phrase, *"Too much of a good thing"*?

Well, it's exactly that!

It's a tough thing to manage, as you don't want to stop your child from doing something they enjoy, but it is also crucial the activity is stopped before problems arise. It's all about reading the signals your child is giving ....

Here are some signs of over-stimulation for you to recognize;

- Sweating
- Panic and crying
- Hysteria – laughing repeatedly
- Lashing out
- Biting
- Loss of balance
- Pale faced
- Child shouting "Stop!"
- Child repeats an irrelevant phrase over and over again
- Nausea

So if you detect any of these 10 signs of over stimulation in your child, ensure you stop the activity as soon as possible. Distract them as best you can onto something else, this way you'll have a better chance of preventing your child from experiencing an overload.

Sensory Integration: Part Three

I can recall, just as if it was yesterday, when I put all my passion into practice and planned my first jam packed one-on-one therapy session for a child that I'd been put in contact with. We had established a great relationship and with Finn's speech difficulties aside, I was confident we'd have a productive session.

I made sure I had a big bag full of different resources with me, as whenever I work with children with autism, I never know what to expect or what might grab their attention. (I must admit it's the challenge of this that keeps me inspired.) Finn's parents told me he loved sensory toys and this was the best way to get his to focus. So I was prepared!

I knocked at the door and waited.

I was welcomed at the door by a very curious, energetic little boy, who, when prompted by his mum, greeted me by using my name, which thrilled me.

I was taken through to the play room where I sat down, dipped into my sensory bag and took out some of my "gems" then I began to play with the toys in front of Finn, over enthusiastically. Squeezing light up balls, laughing at noisy toys, stretching Koosh balls, and "wowing" at flashing toys.

Finn stood by me about a metre away looking out the window.

He was not interested.

So I took out a spinning light up sensory toy (as I was told he loved visual toys) I stared at the different colours and said aloud, "Wow light up toy."

Nope nothing.

Finn was as still as a statue.

The whole time I was playing I kept reminding myself of my own advice, *"keep a positive attitude and a lot of patience and you will see results."*

I looked over at him.

He was now sitting on a small chair gazing around the room. Not exactly the desired reaction I had expected from him.

I remained confident.

"Hey Finn! Look at my light up toy!" I called out.

When I got nothing back, I put the toy back in the bag and turned to face him. He looked towards me and I smiled. Aha! He's watching!

I quickly reached behind my back for a tube of bubbles and started blowing them slowly, Finn was mesmerised, watching each bubble glide slowly and pop on the ground.

"Do you want more bubbles?" I asked him.

"More!" Finn replied urgently.

So I encouraged him to sit beside me, as we the played the "popping" game, and the session had begun!

Like anything in life, some things in the session worked and some things didn't. I decided that I would never let myself become disheartened by the 'bumps in the road'.

Funnily enough, in the end, Finns favourite WAS the light up toy, and while he sat under a blanket, together we enjoyed watching the spinning light.

Finn quickly understood his "reward points" system that I'd set up for him. By the end of our session, he had begun to tick his own chart and understood when it was his reward time.

I thought this was fantastic for our first session.

I thoroughly believe that my consistent positive attitude was a huge factor in the session being successful. Remember that whenever you start something new with your autistic child that not everything will work. Sometimes it's the last thing you try, that can give you the best results...just like the bubbles.

Sensory Integration: Part Four

Many occupational therapists I have worked with over the years, have recommended a 'Sensory diet' for children with autism.

What's a *sensory diet*?

Well, it's a personalised activity plan that has been specifically put together to provide the right balance of sensory input a person needs throughout their day. It has been named a 'sensory diet' to show that just as our children need food and drink throughout the day, they also need the right balance of sensory input to remain focused and alert.

As autistic children can have hyperacute sensory systems, where they can be easily overwhelmed by environmental changes, like loud noises. Or hypoacute sensory systems, where their body requires huge amounts of effort to be alert and engaged.

It's so important that your child's sensory diet is specific to them or it could have the opposite affect to what they are seeking out.

We all have our own ways to help ourselves stay focused. I need to sit in total silence to focus. Whereas my partner Drew, paces around when he's trying to concentrate.

So do you see my point?

We all engage in these types of activities and our children with autism need to engage in stabilising activities too. It is our job as their parents and carers to guide them to the appropriate activities through a sensory diet.

But looking at the wider picture for a minute here, anyone who deals with sensory sensitivities or in-balance can benefit from a personalised sensory diet also. These programmes are not specific to ASD.

As with everything regarding autism, each child has a unique set of sensory needs, tolerances and intolerances.

But generally, a child whose sensory system leaves them "low or lethargic" needs more arousing alternatives to even out their system. And children whose sensory systems leave them "high or hyper" need more calming alternatives.

Occupational therapists can put together a specific personalised Sensory diet for your child. And if it's used right, as part of your child's everyday life, you could see some pretty great results. Below are just a few of the changes you could see in your child from following a personalised sensory diet:

- Able to tolerate sensations and situations they once found challenging

- Regulate their alertness

- Increase attention span

- Minimise sensory seeking and sensory avoiding behaviours

- Handle transitions with ease

If you don't currently have access to an OT, it may be worth taking a look into a few pre-made sensory diets and also at what activities your child may benefit from. This way they can have a taster of a sensory diet and begin exploring different ways to meet their sensory needs daily.

Sensory Integration: Part Five

Self-regulation for children with autism is something that I would describe as "easier said than done". When feeling overwhelmed, many children with autism struggle to seek out appropriate self-regulation and this can, unfortunately, lead to a sensory meltdown. It's imperative that we, as their parents and carers, show our children how to self-regulate to give them the best chance of controlling their sensory sensitivities. When a sensory meltdown occurs, it is important to remove your child from the intolerable sensory input and replace it with something calming.

A great way of helping autistic children self-regulate is by providing them with a 'sensory bag'. Sensory bags can be created and used at home, school or when out and about.

Sensory bags should be unique to your child and contain items that will calm them. But if you're stuck, here are some examples as to what you could have in your child's sensory bag:

- ✔ Soft toy
- ✔ Squeeze ball
- ✔ Koosh ball
- ✔ Sunglasses
- ✔ A hat
- ✔ Fragranced lip balm
- ✔ Ear phones to listen to calming music
- ✔ Bubble wrap
- ✔ Carton of juice (with a straw)
- ✔ Change of clothes (loose hoodie or jumper)

- Chew bar or chewy snack
- Small pot of play-dough
- Bubbles

If you're at home, the same items plus a few other helpful resources can be used. Here are a few suggestions:

- A Mini-trampoline
- Bosu
- Exercise ball
- Weighted blanket or vest
- Hand or foot massage
- Deep pressure massage
- Play slime
- Putty
- Small inside tent
- Rocking chair
- Giant bubbles (to be used outside)
- A swing
- Climbing frame or net

Many of these items are inexpensive or you can create them yourselves. Why not spend the afternoon making your own playdoh? This way it will last longer and you can even make an edible batch.

Sensory Integration Q&A's

"I'm a nanny for a family who have a little boy with autism. Everyday I have to take him out to pick up his older brother from school. The whole time we are out, he covers his ears and shouts out. I think it's because the roads there and the school playground where we pick up his brother are noisy. But how can I get him to stop doing it?"

I understand your situation totally. I was a nanny, many years back and was in exactly the same position as you. Although back then, there wasn't anyone to help me. I am so happy I can offer some personal advice on this one.

It seems that because of the noisy route that you take to school combined with the busy playground, that he is feeling overstimulated and very uncomfortable in this environment. The way he's showing this, is by making noises himself and covering his ears in an attempt to block out what's going on around him. Like many autistic children, he is experiencing hyperacute sensory sensitivities.

If possible, try and find a less noisy route that you could take on the school run. Or alternatively, you could wait outside the school playground until just before you have to go in to collect the brother. This way you're limiting the amount of time he spends in this noisy / busy environment.

Or another quick tip: Give him some earphones and put on some calming music to help him relax during this period. And eventually, fade this back so he doesn't become reliant on it.

"My son has Autism; he was diagnosed late – at 8 years old. He is now 9 and a big boy. We are just learning about the different therapies and resources that can help our son. He has always been very sensory seeking and regularly gets upset and overwhelmed by bright lights, busy places, loud

noises etc. We used to put him in the shopping trolley at the supermarket to help calm him but he's far too big now. He really enjoys physical activity, this seems to calm him. Could you help us out and advise us on how to support our son please?"

Okay great, thanks for all the background info. I'm sorry to hear your son had such a late diagnosis. But let's work with what we know now. Two things scream out to me here and that's...

1. Your son is sensory seeking and hasn't yet found the right self-regulation as he gets overwhelmed a lot in public places.

And,

2. That he enjoys physical activity.

I would advise that you schedule some time in your week for some physical play time with your son. Look out for an outdoor adventure playground with a zip wire perhaps, mazes, sensory garden sand, and sensory rooms. All of these would be great for your son to get out and about, to get his body moving and for him to find the right balance of sensory input that he is seeking. Some special schools and units allow the public to access their sensory rooms, so this may be something to look into for your son.

If you have the space, perhaps invest in a trampoline or small jungle gym for the garden or even a miniature indoor trampoline. These work very well. If he is seeking out physical activities at home, he then has something he can access.

As for your concern about the supermarket, I always say to parents and carers with autistic children to have patience and a positive mindset when raising their children, but I also tell them one other thing, and that's to "pick your battles". You may want to avoid the situation entirely if it makes him very upset and opt to shop online and have your groceries delivered instead.

"I have a 5-year-old daughter who has a diagnosis of autism and she also has other complex needs. Recently she has been hitting herself in the jaw with her fist and with objects. She does it up to 5/6 times an hour and she clenches her teeth as she does this. My wife and I took her to a dentist originally as we thought she might have pain in her teeth. We were told nothing was wrong with our daughter's teeth. The hitting continued and we've since taken her to a doctor who wasn't helpful at all and said it was her "autism". We understand it's likely to be a sensory issue. Is there anything you can advise? Is this something you've seen before?"

I can really relate to this question as I worked with a little boy that engaged in similar behaviours. It's so disappointing and frustrating when other professionals don't take autistic children's health problems seriously, so I'm sorry to hear that you've experienced this. I would always suggest that if you can, get a private specialist doctor.

It's a difficult one, as your child can't express what is making them feel uncomfortable then it could be a range of things, such as;

- Headache
- Tooth pain
- Mouth ulcers
- Abscess
- Migraine
- Jaw ache

And I'm sure there are many others that could potentially be upsetting your child, so it's worth going to a doctor to get your daughter checked over. If you can rule out any health problems, then you can deal with it as a sensory issue.

In which case, if she is hitting herself with her fists and with objects you first need to think about her safety. And as this is a harmful behaviour you'll need to replace it with a safer alternative. I'd suggest a chewy snack such as a granola bar or a chew toy. Fruit flavoured or plain ice cubes will also give your daughter the same sensation. If you see her trying to hit her jaw again, gently block her from doing so and give her the alternative straight away.

"I have a 4 and a half-year-old son who has autism. He goes through phases of different obsessive behaviours. He has most recently become obsessed with playing with his saliva. This phase is going on for longer than usual and he has been engaging in saliva play at home and also when out.

He spits in his mouth and then watches the saliva as he spreads it on any surface that's close to him. This is a such an inappropriate behaviour and I really want to him to stop doing it, but I don't know where to start, can you help?"

This sounds like a sensory behaviour to me, so what you need to do is start implementing an appropriate replacement behaviour strategy. This way your child can learn to engage in this replacement behaviour instead but still be getting the same sensory feedback.

The replacement behaviour not only needs to give him the same sensory feedback but it also has to be comparable to playing with his saliva. Or it's likely he won't want to engage in the new behaviour and he will go back to playing with his saliva.

A good replacement would be a chew stick. If worn on a ribbon or string loosely around his neck a chew stick will be just as accessible to your son as his own saliva. You can also quickly and easily redirect him to his chew stick if it looks as though he is going to begin playing with his saliva.

Many pharmacy's sell chew sticks now and many mother/baby stores sell them too. They come in all sorts of colours, patterns, and shapes. Why don't you take your son with you and let him pick out one himself? Or show him pictures in a catalogue first.

Alternatively your son may enjoy the sensory feeling of liquid in his mouth and "swishing", if you think this might be the case, you could introduce a mouthwash. Purchase a mild tasting wash for children and give him the recommended amount twice a day. Let him explore the mouthwash and enjoy the experience.

A Special gift from *The Ambitious Autism Ambassador'*

Before you go any further, make sure you go to www.unlimitedautismsuccess.com/book-resources and claim over £47 worth of additional tools and templates to help you get the very best from your child with autism.

Here's just some of what you'll get:

- Templates and ideas to help you better manage your child's behaviour

- Additional resources to help aid and improve your child's communication

- Helpful hints and tips to make sure your child is getting the support they need at school

- A ton of things you and the family can do to help your child progress socially and form bonds with others.

- And much more...

To get your FREE bonuses go to...
www.unlimitedautismsuccess.com/book-resources *now.*

SECTION FOUR:

SCHOOL

"The best teachers are those who show you where to look, but don't tell you what to see."

~ Alexandra K Trenfor

Introduction to School

I have worked with autistic children in many different schools over the years, and nothing makes me quite as happy as when I find a school that 'gets' an autistic child.

When a school is totally on board with what you're doing with your child, follows the recommended strategies, communicates and wants the very best for your child, it just makes everyone's lives so much easier.

And...

Inevitably the child with autism thrives.

This I'm sure is every parent or carers dream, and mine too. If I had a list of schools in every town that bend over backwards to support autistic children, believe me I'd share it, but sadly, I don't. Which means that sometimes our autistic children don't always receive the support they deserve in school.

Once I worked with a family who had a son on the spectrum, who attended an unsupportive school that did the barest minimum to support his way of learning. One day the emotionally and physically exhausted the mother said to me...

"What more can I do?"

I drew in a breath and told her honestly, "You can fight for the help and support he deserves until the school listens and puts things in place for him, or you can find a new school and potentially have to face this all over again."

My words struck a cord with this parent, and she sprung to life again.

Because it's true.

Every single child deserves the right to reach their full potential and we as parents and carers of autistic children need to stand by this.

A child's success at school is dependent on the teacher's success and the way in which they liaise with parents and other professionals. Partnerships at school are key for an autistic child to meet their full potential.

The social skills which all children learn from being at school is irreplaceable. Learning how to follow rules, make and maintain friendships and play in many different ways are all essential parts of development. And children with autism are no different, although some of these skills may be harder for our children to grasp. But just being in this environment is so important for autistic children. As their social experiences at school will slowly but surely open the door to their own "social thinking."

School: Part One

In the months of January and February in the UK, many of our streets are dusted with a sheet of perfectly white snow. Our roofs, cars, and streets are coated. And unless you attempt to commute to work this means only one thing...

Snow Day!

Now snow days, for anyone unfamiliar with this term, is how we describe a day off work/school because of the snowy conditions, and also to our country for failing to have the resources to clear enough of the snow to enable us to travel. (Even when such weather conditions were predicted on the news weeks before!)

Families gather in parks, making snowmen, throwing snowballs and generally enjoying a day NOT having to go to work or going school!

EVERYONE LOVES A SNOW DAY!

Or do they?

I was born in the summer and have always adored hot weather. So although I like the fact that snow is pretty and it brings families together....

I hate the cold.

In winter, I don't leave my house till I'm wrapped up to the point of sweating! And quite honestly, because I love what I do and I would rather be working on a snow day.

This reminds me of a child I used to work with...

James was 7 years old at the time. He was autistic and had speech delay, and I was supporting him in his mainstream school.

Every Tuesday afternoon straight after the register was taken, the class of 30 would squeeze together on the carpet area for a story.

Every Tuesday afternoon when the teacher said: "Now quietly tuck in your chairs and find a space on the carpet for story time." The class would burst into smiles and make, "Yesssss" celebrations to one another.

All except for James.

Every Tuesday James would glue himself to his chair and anxiously squeeze his fingers and thumbs together, looking in my direction.

James did this because he hated story time the same way I hated the cold.

At first, when I explained this to the teacher she struggled to understand. "But he is able to relax comfortably on the carpet during story time and nobody is expecting anything from him." She said.

She didn't realise that...being expected to sit in a different place each week, expected to be silent, expected to allow 29 other bodies close to him AND expected to listen without understanding the story (as the books were too complex)....

...was, in fact, a HUGE expectation!

After I had explained this properly, I went to work, quickly setting up a plan to help James feel more at ease during story time.

So there I was at 4:00pm sitting in my silent, empty classroom, 30 minutes after the infamous 'end of school' bell had rung, where hundreds of children raced to their freedom outside the school gates. I was sitting there racking my brain as to how I was going to help James 'enjoy' story time.

To be quite honest at times I questioned whether I was doing the right thing.

But I had to remind myself that at this stage I wasn't expecting James to like story time, but simply tolerate it without feeling anxious. I knew big changes needed to happen for James to achieve this goal and I was up for the challenge!

I set out writing down some bullet points on what James had found difficult about story time.

- Sharing his space
- Choosing a different space on the carpet each week
- Remaining engaged in the story
- Sitting still

Then I brainstormed ideas for each point and wrote down the most practical and efficient strategies.

Here was my list:

- Sharing his space -> Introducing "wave space" to the whole class
- Choosing a different space on the carpet each week -> James having a corner to choose from rather than a spot and to make others aware of his corner
- Remaining engaged in the story -> Creating flash card questions to hold up to the class after each main event
- Sitting still -> Taking advantage of James's rubber obsession

I gathered the necessary resources, packed them away and made my way home...

...thinking of James the whole way.

Tuesday came around quickly and I was keen to put my plan for James into action.

Before lunchtime I took James outside the classroom to explain the new rules for story time.

Inside the classroom, the class teacher spoke to the rest of the class about 'James' corner' she told them that only six children could be in the same corner as James at one time.

Outside, I told James that we had put together some new rules for story time so that it would be more fun! James nodded and bit his lip, listening intently to what I was saying. Next I told him that he could choose a corner on the carpet and that every single Tuesday we would make sure he got his space in the same corner.

He smiled and nodded.

One thing I haven't told you about James was his obsession with rubbers. James had a small pencil case on his desk in which he kept all his rubbers, big rubbers, small rubbers, animal rubbers, vehicle rubbers, letter rubbers...

...and the list goes on, James adored rubbers!

So when I told James he could choose ONE of his favourite rubbers each Tuesday afternoon to hold whilst on the carpet...He was overjoyed.

Together, James and I went back into the classroom and joined the others. The teacher then told everyone that at each story time they all needed to have enough space around them and instructed them to stretch out their arms and wave.

The whole class then practiced.

She went on to say that she would be holding up "Quiz Questions" to the class during parts of the story and whoever got the question correct, would receive a "star point."

The classroom filled with "ohhhhhhhh's" and "aahhhhhhh's"

James joined in.

The class was then dismissed for their lunch.

After lunch, I went down to the playground to collect the class. James was standing at the front of the line, as he always did.

"It's story time now, register first, then story." He informed me.

I was happy with his enthusiasm as he had never mentioned story time to me before.

I walked with the children to our classroom and as quick as a flash James was at his desk searching his "rubber pencil case" for the perfect one!

Then James heard a familiar sound....

"Now quietly tuck in your chairs and find a space on the carpet for story time." The teacher announced.

And instead of the usual 'gluing himself to his chair and anxiously squeezing his fingers and thumbs together, looking in my direction.'

James smiled at his sheep rubber...walked slowly towards me...And without a prompt James pointed to the carpet and said, "That corner."

I nodded in acceptance and James sat down in his desired spot.

And the rest is history!

By the third story time, with our new rules, James was sitting happily for the duration of story time AND even answering the odd 'quiz question'. Proof that sometimes a few new strategies, an open mind and a whole lot of consistently being patient, can have amazing results!

School: Part Two

Many parents and carers of autistic children struggle with gaining and holding their child's attention when interacting with them and I can say from experience this is a challenge that can be very frustrating.

There are 100's of factors you have to think about when trying to solve this. For example:

- Did they actually hear you?

- Do they understand the language you're using?

- Did you make your expectation clear?

- Would a visual aid help?

- Is there a motivation for them to interact with you?

- What are they getting out of the situation?

And so on and so on.

One of the things I touched upon above was visual aids. Now IF you use visual aids correctly, they can be a fantastic way of promoting language at school. But unfortunately if they are used incorrectly, your child can become so dependent on them, that it will have the reverse effect.

And another thing...

There are SO many types of visuals available, that you can easily feel like you don't know where to start and that you're fighting a losing battle.

But I assure you, you are not!

When you're struggling to gain your child's attention, it's hard to remember that many children with autism have a shorter attention span than neuro-typical children. Therefore, concentrating for long periods of time can actually be a real challenge for them!

One thing that I and many other autism professionals have found to be a life saver in overcoming this hurdle of concentration, are 'Fidget toys'.

Research has shown that children with autism who have a short attention span, can focus much better, just by having something in their hands to fiddle with.

Fidget toys can be easily purchased online and in a range of stores. They can range from a slinky, a koosh, to a squeezy toy and they don't have to be expensive. . Something even as simple as a stone or shell can work wonders.

Or...

If you're feeling creative why not make a fidget toy at home with your child. Creative play is great relaxation therapy for autistic children. How about a pipe cleaner monster or an animal made from aluminium foil, a bubble wrap ball or even a colourful glitter shaker?

School: Part Three

Last year I witnessed something amazing...It was one of those moments where I couldn't take my eyes off what I was watching. My heart melted, my eyes welled up and I was smiling so much my jaw ached!

I was working in a ASD school at the time and it was a Friday. Friday afternoons at this school, like many other schools had 'golden time'.

For anyone unfamiliar with the term 'golden time', it's basically a time when children have free play. And in this particular school, there were themed rooms with different activities and the children could choose which room they wanted to play in for the afternoon.

I was supervising in the relaxation room, along with a few other members of staff. The usual children joined us each week, our 'regulars' I called them. They were mainly children with limited language and that struggled with social interaction. They came into to the relaxation room to shut off.

And why not, it was 'their time' after all!

One child, in particular, stood out in the room, mainly because he was making quite a lot of noise. Ben was shouting to himself and throwing a squeeze ball rhythmically into the air...He wasn't bothering anyone so we let him be.

I watched him throw the squeeze ball as I tried to work out what he was shouting.

Then a member of staff went over and sat near him. She smiled and watched him happily throwing and shouting, throwing and shouting.

All the while Ben hadn't taken his gaze off his squeeze ball to acknowledge her.

She reached into a toy box and pulled out a red squeeze ball just like Ben's...

She threw her ball in the air and suddenly shouted...

"CHARMANDER!!"

Ben stopped throwing.

He stared her in the face, slightly frowning.

She looked back with an inviting smile...then...Ben threw his ball into the air...

"BULBASAUR!!" he yelled, staring at the stranger.

The Pokémon enthusiast threw her squeeze ball again,

"PIKACHU!!" she added smiling.

Ben stared then began to throw his ball again.

Ben and his new play partner continued to play this game non-stop for two more minutes before the bell rang to signal the end of 'golden time'.

I must admit I was a little disappointed when the game had to end. Watching them play together and listening to Ben speaking continuously with another person was nothing short of incredible. Plus I learnt heaps of Pokémon names, which amused me!

After we'd tidied up the relaxation room, as Ben's new play buddy was leaving, she walked towards me .

I had to tell her, "That was amazing watching you with Ben. The whole six months I've been at this school I've never seen him interact like that." I blurted out to her, smiling.

She looked over at Ben...

"Pokémon was 'my thing' growing up, I guess it's Ben's 'thing' too!" she said to me smiling back.

Here is a perfect example of someone making the effort to tap into an autistic child's interest and joining them there. All too often we and myself included expect our child with autism to engage in something they either don't yet understand or have no interest in. Then we feel bad if they don't communicate with us.

Well, first things first...Don't feel bad for doing this.

It can feel weird or even pointless engaging in an autistic child's play, but stay with it and explore their interests, gain their trust and you never know where it will lead.

School: Part Four

I remember when I learnt to ride a bike...

Almost everyone where I lived was learning or could already ride one so I felt more than ready to start. My Gran had bought me this pink and silver bike with a white basket and stabilisers.

I loved it!

No seriously, I stared at it for a whole minute with a huge (slightly weird) grin on my face when I first got it.

I was ready to ride!

Where I lived at the time, there was a nearby grass area with a pathway going around the outside. That was where I first began to learn...I went happily round and round the green.

Piece of cake.

The only thing was, I couldn't ride fast enough!

I saw some of the other children out on their bikes that week. But they didn't use stabilisers.

That was it....I wanted them off!

I was clearly a natural at riding so I'd coped just fine without stabilisers. I remember my dad telling me I'd be fine, it was all about balance and focus.

I got this, I thought.

Not that I really understood what he meant by that.

So a few days later I had my stabilisers taken off and I was back on that pathway again ready to ride for real this time.

Wow!

Let's just say I totally underestimated how difficult it was going to be. Like most children I fell off and got back on to try again...

Many times.

From a very young age I've had a determined streak in me, so getting back on my bike after falling off felt like my only option.

I had to learn and sure as hell wasn't giving up!

It's just like when you teach something new to an autistic child.

It will be hard when you first start out...BUT...if you focus on your goal and not the set backs, your child will achieve so much more.

And if it takes six, seven or eight tries, guess what...the same thing applies!

Dust yourself off and try again. I'm not saying it will be easy but it will definitely be worthwhile. If you stay positive and focused on your desired outcome, you'll get there.

School: Part Five

I once listened to an Anthony Robbins personal development audio. Aside from the obvious life changing, motivating and inspirational stuff you learn, there was one other thing Anthony said that stuck out in my head....

Oh and by the way! If you've never listened to any of his stuff I'd highly recommend you do, his audios are all full of ideas that are bound to help you and your whole family!

Anyway...He talked about the power of *"asking the right questions."*

Robbins strongly believes that: "Quality questions create a quality life."

You see, everyone asks themselves questions in life.

You know the ones...

"Why did that happen to me?"

"What was I thinking?"

"What am I supposed to do now?"

Well, what Robbins teaches is to tweak our questions just a little, so that our questions are positive and they empower us.

For example instead of saying...."What am I happy about in my life today?"

You would say, *"What could I be happy about in my life today?"*

Can you see how just a small tweak can change the whole question entirely?

Well, this concept got me thinking....

Children spend so much of their time at school and sometimes it can feel like we know so little about what goes on when they're there.

That's why it's so important to ask the right questions when you meet with or communicate with your child's teachers.

But just like Anthony Robbins says, sometimes we don't ask the right questions.

And then we're left frustrated and feeling like we're in the dark.

Have you ever felt 'in the dark' about what goes on when your child is at school?

Do you worry about your child having meltdowns or feeling anxious at school?

Do you wish you knew more about how your child is getting on at school?

Well, let me help you.

I've come up with six questions that are designed specifically to help YOU find out more, feel more in the loop and learn ways to help your child progress at school, so take note;

- ✔ Question1) What progress has my child made this year at school?

- ✔ Question 2) What are my child's biggest challenges in the class setting?

- ✔ Question 3) What areas can I work on at home to help my child progress?

- ✔ Question 4) Does my child show any anxiety during their school day? If yes, what do you think this is triggered by?

And finally, possibly the most important question of them all...

- ✔ Question 5) Is there anything else I need to know

regarding my child at school?

Now, let me tell you why question 5 is the most important.

I have worked alongside teachers, both mainstream, ASD and special needs for over a decade now, and more often than not, these teachers struggle to give negative feedback to parents of autistic children.

Yeah, I said it!

I went there!

But it's true.

And don't get me wrong I'm not slating teachers here.

Who likes giving negative feedback to someone?

It's tough,

It's uncomfortable.

It may even turn out confrontational.

Teachers aren't super heroes, they struggle with stuff too, just like you and I!

But, it is *essential* that you know exactly what's going on with your child while they're at school. Because then and only then, can you work on any challenges they might be facing.

Communication, recall, relaying information and social interactions are notoriously challenging for children with autism.

So it's easy for parents and carers of autistic children to feel 'in the dark' about how their child is getting on at school.

That's exactly why that when you're at a parents evening or any other type of school meeting regarding your child you ask the question;

Is there anything else I need to know regarding my child at school?

This question not only hands it over to the teacher, but it has a *"tell me the good, the bad and the ugly"* feel to it.

By saying, *"is there anything...."?* You're telling the teacher it doesn't matter what it is, you just want to know.

This way they are more likely to share, rather than if you ask in a more aggressive direct way.

So make sure you make a mental note of question 5 and have it ready for your next school meeting.

School Q&A's

"I teach children aged 4/5 years old and I've been told my next class (which I'll be teaching in two months time) will have 2 autistic children in it. I'm nervous as I am only in my second year of teaching and I haven't yet taught a child with autism. I've expressed my concerns to my line manager but she wasn't very supportive at all. I want to make sure I am able to meet their needs in the classroom and include them the best I can. How do you suggest I do this, please help?"

Firstly if you haven't met these two children yet, then you can't possibly know their needs and how to include them in your class. I can understand it's scary as it's a new challenge for you, but I think you're worrying about things you are unsure of. It's normal for us to worry about the unknown. I'd strongly advise you to do some research into some "Introduction to Autism" type courses. Once you've got a basic understanding, you will feel a lot more confident about your new class situation. Personally, I'd run the course by your line manager to see if they will fund it as career/ personal development.

Secondly, if your two new autistic children have both been diagnosed, then it's likely they are eligible for one-on-one support. Which will take some of the stress off you when you're teaching the whole class. This is something else I would look into and speak to your line manager/SENCO about. One-on-one support is a fantastic tool for autistic children to access as many activities in school as possible and thrive.

"I work in a mainstream school with 6 and 7-year-olds and right now there is a child with autism in my class. He fits in the class really well and the other children are very patient and kind towards him. But I am struggling with some of his behaviours. I have worked with autistic children before but I have never taught a child this old who doesn't sit in his

chair. This boy is very disruptive as he is out of his chair and walking around the room in the middle of lessons and carpet time and I don't know how to keep him sitting? Please, can you help?"

I'd suggest that you modify your expectation for the child with autism in you class. For example, take carpet time, if you usually spend 15 minutes doing carpet times with your class, only expect the child with autism to sit and engage for five to six minutes of this. After this have one of your teaching aids take him to another area of the room for a short break or let him take part in a less challenging activity. Make sure you take him back to the carpet during the last three minutes when you give the class the instruction.

I'd also suggest that you look at how you are delivering your teaching. For example;

Do you provide times for your children to move around or jump about?

Are your modifying tasks so that the child with autism is able to complete them?

Is your teaching always delivered in an auditory manner? Are you also teaching in visual and tactile ways?

Do you tailor your language when you give an instruction to the child with autism to ensure they really understand you?

These are some factors I'd look into. And finally, make it fun! Who said teaching couldn't be fun? The more engaged children are, the more they are likely to absorb.

"I have a child with autism in my class at the moment and myself and his one-on-one are really struggling with him, particularly at home time. For the majority of the day, we have his behaviour under control and his needs are being met, which is fab. But at home time, just before his mother comes to pick him up, he gets very anxious. He shouts out, lies on the ground and cries. When his mum actually comes

in to get him, he's extremely violent towards her. I feel helpless, what would you advise?"

I think in your situation it's essential that you prepare him for home time. Although I'm sure you have a standard home time routine as all schools will, but I think he needs a personalised one.

Bur firstly if you haven't already, I'd speak with his mum. Ask her why she thinks this behaviour may be happening. It may be that he is going through some difficulties at home and if so, it's important you are aware of this.

Next start collecting some photos for a personalised social story, get photos of yourself, of his bag, his coat, the classroom, a few of his classmates, the area of where he gets picked up and also photos of any adults who pick him up. Put together a simple social story explaining what's going to happen at the end of each day. Repeat the phrase "this is okay" throughout the story. This will help ease any anxiety. Also, explain the concept of having still and calm hands and feet during home time, fidget toys may help with this. Read the story to him or have one of your teaching aides read it to him right before the routine begins. If the child begins to shout or drop to the floor at any time, sit next to him and calmly read or offer a fidget toy.

You may want to set up a reward system with his mother (or whoever else picks him up) whereby when he gets five stickers for good behaviour during the home time routine, she can give him a reward. A trip to the park on the way home for example.

Make sure of two things;

1) The reward is given to him by his mother (or whoever picks him up), not by you or any other teacher.

This is essential because this will help stop the violence towards his mother.

2) That the reward is given to him straight away.

If the reward is a trip to the park, this should happen straight from school. Or if it's time to play a game on a tablet, then the tablet can be brought to the school pick-up by mum.

This is important because when the correct behaviour is reinforced instantly, the child is much more likely to repeat that behaviour again.

"I am a teacher and I have two autistic children in my class. It's very difficult to get both children to sit and engage during school assemblies with his peers. They try to get up and run around. I have two support staff, but if they chase the boys, they tend to find this funny and if they sit with them, they enjoy the attention and still play up. I'm unsure of what to do and my staff are feeling helpless. What can I do to get them to sit and engage the same way the rest of the class does?"

I've personally dealt with and also seen this happen in many schools, so you're not on your own with this. The way I dealt with disengagement and eloping during school assemblies was by modifying the time which they are sitting. For example:-

Would they concentrate more if they were given more sitting space?

Or would they concentrate more if they had a fiddle toy?

Is it essential that they spend the whole 20 minutes in the school assembly? Or could they be taken out five minutes before the end?

Are they being reinforced for their good sitting?

Is the floor they're sitting on making them uncomfortable and therefore promoting this behaviour?

I think when it comes to things like this it's important to look at them through the autistic child's point of view. And also "pick your battles" if you make some changes and their sitting in school assemblies improves but fades out towards the end, take them out! If it's for the sake of three or four minutes of school announcements is it really worth it?

A Special gift from *'The Ambitious Autism Ambassador'*

Before you go any further, make sure you go to www.unlimitedautismsuccess.com/book-resources and claim over £47 worth of additional tools and templates to help you get the very best from your child with autism.

Here's just some of what you'll get:

- Templates and ideas to help you better manage your child's behaviour
- Additional resources to help aid and improve your child's communication
- Helpful hints and tips to make sure your child is getting the support they need at school
- A ton of things you and the family can do to help your child progress socially and form bonds with others.
- And much more...

To get your FREE bonuses go to...
www.unlimitedautismsuccess.com/book-resources *now.*

SECTION FIVE:

FAMILY LIFE

"A happy family is but an earlier heaven."

~ George Bernard Shaw

Introduction to Family Life

I believe when you have a child with autism living in your home you need to have the following:

- ✔ Strategy
- ✔ Consistency
- ✔ Positivity
- ✔ Fun

Now let me explain why I believe this.

If you do not have a plan for when a meltdown occurs or change in routine or a specific challenging behaviour, for example eloping, then when the inevitable happens you will be forced to make it up as you go along.

Or as I say, "wing it."

You see the problem, with "winging it" with an autistic child, is it almost never works out. Unless by a stroke of luck you have everything you need and your 'on the spot' plan works, the behaviour will escalate.

But, by having a clear strategy for these situations that you know works, you can manage the situation, instead of just winging it.

Having a strategy is great but if everyone in your home is not on the same page, unfortunately, you won't get very far. That's why consistency is the next thing on my list. Having everyone on board, I mean, siblings, grandparents, teachers, aunts, uncles is the best way. Break down your strategy, make it easy for them to understand and enforce that it is the best thing for your son or daughter.

Even on those harder days, the sleepy, not feeling yourself days...

...yes even on those days, stick with the strategy!

Because being consistent is vital to having a more relaxed and fulfilled home life with your child.

Number three is positivity. I've touched upon the importance of positive reinforcement with autistic children many times, because it plays such a big role in autistic behaviours. And this again is also something you need to think about doing at home with your child.

But I'm talking about a different type of positivity right now.

Having a positive mind is, in my opinion, a very powerful tool! Focusing on positives rather than negatives could be the difference between having a great day or a terrible day. And it's the same when raising children with autism. If you think about all the things you've tried that have failed and how you just don't know what to do in a situation, then one thing will happen...

...you WON'T discover how at all!

Positive thinking opens all kinds of doors in life. Try to adapt your mind to think and focus on the positives and then watch how this new thinking will seep into your relationship with your autistic child and your entire family.

And last of all, have fun! So much of the time on TV, in news articles and radio shows we hear about the struggles children and families have who live with autism, a dark cloud appears over our heads and all of a sudden everything turns gloomy.

I'm here to say, let's step away from that gloominess. Let's have fun with our autistic children! All children love to have fun, to run, jump, laugh and play let's encourage and accompany our children.

If your child is feeling particularly sensory seeking one morning, get the messy play out or do hand or foot printing with them. If they are jumping and running around the house one afternoon, Google your nearest adventure playground, prepare them and go have fun with them! If it's raining and they are at a loose end, build a den with them, take torches inside or listen to relaxing music.

An ASD diagnosis does not mean no fun, so get out there and enjoy your time with your child.

Family Life: Part One

Autistic traits vary from one child to another, but something many autistic children have in common, is their love of predictability. There's something about predictability that makes autistic children feel safe and 'in the loop' if you like.

So many parents and carers I've spoken to have said that they wished their child was more 'present' and so by encouraging their love or need for predictability is a great way of achieving this.

A fun and lovely way of doing this is by exposing autistic children to repetitive language stories. I'm talking about Jack and the Beanstalk, The Three Little Pigs and The Ginger Bread Man type of stories. All the stories that use repetitive language throughout the book. For example, the phrase, "Fee-fi-fo-fum" in Jack and the Beanstalk and "I'll huff and I'll puff" in the three little pigs.

Read these stories with your child at appropriate times, just before bed as a calming activity is perfect. Make sure that you put emphasis on the recurring parts to promote communication. E.g. "So what did the giant say...?" Once you've found a story that your child loves, reading is sure to be a rewarding and positive activity that will bring the two of you closer together.

If your child becomes obsessed with one particular story, that is okay, just make sure you ration that particular book. For example, that can be the story for Tuesday nights only.

If appropriate after a couple of times of reading the book, tell your child you'll be taking turns in reading the story. Stop at the repetitive phrases as a clear indication that it's their turn to finish the phrase. When they do, be sure to applaud and give them lots of positive praise. I'd advise that any older or more verbal siblings do not join in on this activity in case they are tempted to fill in the gaps. Give your autistic child the time they need to speak without interruptions. When they're confident in filling in the phrases, then you can feel free to invite other family members to join in and then all huddle up in the bed together to read.

If you're looking for some more 'up to date' repetitive language stories here are a few fabulous examples that I love to use:

'Room on the Broom' & 'Stick Man' by Julia Donaldson

'Brown Bear Brown Bear' by Bill Martin and Eric Carl

'Dear Zoo' by Rod Campbell

'Good Night, Gorilla' by Peggy Rathmann

Family Life: Part Two

A few years ago whilst travelling through London on a bus, I saw something happen that caught my attention and really made me think about the way we talk to children with autism.

I was engrossed in one of my favourite books when a little boy caught my eye....

He was about two years old, he was sitting up in his push chair with his mum standing beside him. And next, to them was another mother with her child, only in this push chair was a tiny baby, no more than a month or two old.

The two-year-old boy, who I will call Michael, was absolutely covered in ketchup from the chips his mum was feeding him. As I watched Michael, I noticed how curiously he was looking at the newborn baby in the pram next to him.

And I suddenly felt a little strange...

Have you ever had that feeling when you can just tell something funny is about to happen?

Michael was now completely staring at the newborn baby and at this point he was pointing at her and looking back at his mum. Who was looking at her phone and wasn't paying any attention to the situation.

Michael then sat himself forward in his push chair to get a better look at his new friend. He stared at her for about another 30 seconds or so, getting as close to her face as possible.

At this point, that funny feeling was getting stronger in the bottom of my stomach.

Then suddenly Michael caved and gave in to his curiosity, he reached out and touched the baby's face. Michael's mother bounced back to life and quickly slapped away his hand shouting.

"No! Don't touch the baby your hands are filthy!"

Michael frowned at his mum looking shocked and very confused. I understood his confusion and I could tell I was looking at his mum in the same way. I mean...What is she really telling her son?

Not to touch newborn babies he doesn't know when his hands are dirty?

Or not to touch them at all?

Was it okay to touch a baby if his hands were clean?

I thought to myself, if I was confused about what she meant and her son Michael was confused about what she meant, how on earth would a child with autism make sense of it? (Assuming here that Michael wasn't on the spectrum)

We have to be so careful how we explain things to autistic children. As parents and carers, we are the first educators of our children and what they hear from us first will stick in their little heads.

I personally remember as a small child my dad told me that Jesus lived in heaven and that heaven was in the sky. So the first time I went on a plane, I was ecstatic! I excitedly asked my dad if I could sit by the window so I could look out for Jesus!

Now, what my dad said was a silly comment that ended in laughter, but remember that children with autism are often very logical thinkers. So it's important we are clear about what we mean when we speak to our autistic children.

Or as my dad used to say, "Think before you speak!"

Family Life: Part Three

Over the years, I've worked with many autistic children who have what I call the "I can't syndrome."

These are the types of children that don't yet have the confidence to challenge themselves. Many people feel this way about trying new things and that's okay. But I live by the mantra that you do it anyway, otherwise, you don't progress. So, it's time for our "I can't" children to stop holding themselves back and make some positive changes!

A fun, innovative and non-pushy way of helping them to do this, is to create an 'I can't' time capsule with your child and stage a burial.

Sound crazy?

Let me explain what I mean by this;

- First, your child will write down all their 'I can't's', or you can do that for them. Spend some time on this part so that you don't miss anything out. Ensure that your child knows this is a fun activity rather than a 'telling off', make it exciting, tell them it's an adventure, a journey to the future.

- Next tear or cut out all their 'I can't's' and place them all into a lunchbox or jar.

- Then gather together your team/crew or fellow cadets and find an appropriate place to stash or bury your capsule. This can be the whole family, class or even an independent activity, whatever's most comfortable for your child.

- Finally, decide on the length of time you will leave your capsule and tell your child. Mark the date on your family calendar.

What you will discover when the capsule is uncovered, is that many of the 'I can't's' have become 'I can's'! If done correctly, it's an amazing way of documenting your child's progress and showing them how proud you are of their accomplishments, and building their confidence and self-worth in order to challenge themselves in the future.

Just ensure that the length of time is enough to see substantial changes, as there's nothing worse for your child's self-esteem than identifying unachieved goals.

Have fun and create a capsule with your child today, and who knows you may even want to slip in a few for yourself!

Family Life: Part Four

Children with Autism find expressing their emotions extremely challenging. And when it comes to anger it is no different. Sometimes when autistic children express themselves in a negative or aggressive way, through screaming, hitting, kicking, verbal insults or head banging, these behaviours show, that your child is frustrated.

Understandably as a parent you just want to help your child feel OKAY again, right?

Well, once you've identified what emotion your child is feeling and their need, you are one step closer to helping them.

The next step is to decide on an appropriate calming technique that your child can do by themselves for approximately a minute to ease their frustration. For example, jump on the trampoline, pop or stamp on bubble wrap, hit a punching bag or their pillow.

After these steps are in place it would be a great idea to make up a short and simple "social story" about being frustrated or angry. Use language your child will understand and write in short, clear sentences. You can make it into a small booklet if you think your child will respond better.

Here is a simple outline of a "social story" based on a child feeling angry or frustrated.

→ My name is _____

→ Just like everyone else, sometimes I feel angry.

→ It is OKAY to feel angry.

→ When I feel angry, I can jump on my trampoline.

→ This will help me feel better

→ When I am finished jumping, I will feel happy again.

You will introduce the social story to your child when they are calm, read through it with them and share ideas. (Preferably do this more than once) Then whenever you can see your child beginning to feel angry or frustrated, you will give them their story to read themselves. Or if your child cannot read you can read it to them.

Be sure to make the social story look appealing to your child, use real life pictures throughout the book. You can even add in pictures of their favourite cartoon character to encourage them to read it... In some cases, children have responded well to seeing photos of their face pulling an angry and happy expression or you can use your child's own drawings with captions. Explore what works best for your child.

Family Life: Part Five

It is so easy to get swept away by our busy schedules and the everyday roller-coaster of life. Remembering to visit a friend, call your sister back, buy bin bags or fill up your car with petrol before you get home.

Sound familiar?

Of course you're only human, we all feel like this sometimes. But it's important that we pay close attention to how we communicate with our children when we feel like this.

Often when we talk to our children, we forget to gain contact with them before we start to communicate.

And what's more, we do this and then expect them to take on board what we're saying!

It is essential for parents and carers of autistic children to make an effort to gain the attention of your child before initiating any kind of conversation.

Autistic children often have weaker social referencing abilities than typically functioning children, which means if we just talk "at them" we are potentially overwhelming them and making the experience something highly uncomfortable...

And, like the old saying goes; *"It will go in one ear and out the other!"*

Always ensure that when beginning a conversation with your child you are at their eye level. This is crucial, even if your child doesn't give you eye contact straight away. Sitting or squatting next to them will make the world of difference compared to shouting something to them from the other side of the room.

Once you're next to them and at their eye level, you now need to let the child know that you are about to communicate with them and this commands their attention. It sounds simple but it's something we take for granted because we do understand these social questions. But remember these skills often do not come naturally for children with autism.

This step sounds harder than it is, a simple tap on the shoulder or touch to their chin (if touch is tolerated) could be all they need. If this doesn't work try a verbal prompt, for example, use their name first or say, "listen Freddie" or, "Freddie watch". Some ASD children may need to hear their name to realise the words they hear are being directed specifically at them.

Also, make sure that any hand gestures you use are appropriate this might sound like a weird thing to say, but hear me out! If a child is used to Makaton at school, and when they go home their parents speak to them using their hands, waving them around for no real reason, this can be highly confusing for your ASD child but it may just simply be a habit for you.

Be mindful of how you communicate to your child, keep it simple. And keep a mental note of what prompts you've used so that you can eventually fade this back.

Family Life: Part Six

We all have trouble sleeping from time to time. You know when you have one of those nights when you can't get comfy...

You can't switch your brain off.

You're constantly thinking about things you need to do or things you're worried about?

And inevitably you wake up feeling pretty lousy. Your body aches and you don't feel well rested at all.

Many children on the spectrum also have trouble with sleep. And this can be a really challenging thing to work on, because there are so many different reasons your child may be struggling with sleeping...

If you are battling with sleep difficulties with your child, one thing to think about is whether or not your child is comfortable.

Now, this may sound super simple, but hear me out because many parents and carers miss this one...*think about it*...

When you pick out a pair of pajamas for yourself, you are looking for something quite specific.

A specific style...

A specific length...

Maybe a specific fabric...

Something you're going to be comfortable in, right?

Well, what if the pajamas you choose for your child aren't comfortable for them?....

What if the long pajama bottoms you chose, gives your child all-over pressure that irritates them?

Or what if the loose baggy style top you picked out constantly rides up or tickles your child?

What if those cool pajamas you got your child drives them nuts, because of the elastic around the wrists and ankles?

Maybe the pretty night dress you found itches and the embroidery rubs on your child's skin?

Something to think about, right?

Because rolling up their trousers, tucking in their tops or telling your child to "just try to go to sleep" might not be enough and may be contributing to their sleep difficulties.

Another thing that may be causing your child to have sleep difficulties is their sleeping space...

Answer these questions now, either out loud, in your head or perhaps on a piece of paper;

→ What type of bed does your child have?

→ Does anything accompany them in their sleeping space?

→ Does your child have boundaries in their sleeping space?

→ And finally, does your child rest well in their sleeping space?

Do your answers show that you need to change your child's sleeping space in some way?

Well, many children with autism feel uneasy in their sleeping space and this can result in sleep difficulties.

Sometimes it may be that their space is too big and they may feel that they have no boundaries.

A great way of getting around this is wrapping up your child in their bed.

You can do this by using a weighted blanket – these are often recommended by Occupational Therapists, but consult your child's OT to discuss this beforehand.

Or another great and easy way to help your child feel boundaries when they're sleeping is by wrapping them up tight in a sleeping bag.

Many children I've worked with enjoy the feeling of being squeezed and wrapped up tight. This can help autistic children relax and feel comforted.

Family Life Q&A's

"Our son is 4 and he has autism, he's had a private therapist for the past two years now and he has made so much progress. His speech is really coming on, he tries new foods much more than he used to, he doesn't get so obsessed by just one toy anymore and he has fewer meltdowns. We are very happy with his progress, but we still really struggle to take him out to eat. His vocal stims are so loud and disruptive in restaurants and he never stays sitting in his chair."

All families are different but I'm sure many families want to take their autistic child out to eat but feel like they can't so you're not on your own with this.

If your son's vocal stims are much louder and disruptive in restaurants than when you're eating at home, then to me this suggests he may be feeling anxious in the restaurant.

Do you tend to go at peak times when it's very busy?

Could you choose a more segregated table?

Does he feel better if he sits by the exit?

Do you think taking a few small sensory toys would help calm his vocal stims?

As for getting out of his seat, this can be practised at home during meal times. I'd advise you to set up a simple star chart of the token board and reward him for every minute of good sitting. Once this behaviour is finally controlled, I'd write a short social story about going out to eat. Make sure it isn't specific to one restaurant or one type of food. Also, make a small laminated card with a picture of something your child likes. For example, I've done this before and used a picture of a rocket. Personally, I prefer a picture rather than a "I need a break" style symbol to keep it relaxed and low key. Explain in the social story that he can show his rocket card if he feels "funny" (use whatever appropriate language your child would understand)

If he shows you the rocket card, you can remind him of the sensory toys he can play with or even take him outside for a two or three minute walk to help him relax. As I said, keep it relaxed to make sure it doesn't feel like your son is in trouble for showing you his card.

And also, practise using the rocket card at home in different situations to make sure he understands and can generalise the concept.

Then once you're ready to go out to eat again, read him the social story, gather together a few calming toys, his rocket card and enjoy! The first time may not be perfect but hey, *"practice makes perfect!"*

"I have a son who is autistic he is 7 years old. He has always had issues with speech, from a young age it was very difficult to motivate him to speak. We tried lots of different things but he is very limited in the things he likes or will work for. I'm afraid that over the years I've prompted him too much with his speech that he is now prompt dependent. But the thing this, if I stop prompting him he doesn't speak at all. Please, can you help?"

Finding the right reinforcements are essential when working on any skill with children who have autism. The right reinforcements needs to be both motivating enough that the child will work hard to get it and appropriate for it to work repeatedly.

For example sweets aren't a good idea to use for a child who has a limited range of reinforcers, they will not work for as you wouldn't want your child to be working for sweets for an entire hour and to rot their teeth!

I'd advise all parents to try to have at least three different reinforcers that they use with their autistic child. This way you won't be stuck if they become unmotivated during a task.

I understand if your child seems as though he has a limited range of things he is interested in that this can be difficult. A great way to learn about what a child with autism is interested in is by simply observing them when they are alone.

Sounds simple, right?

That's because it is. The difficult part is taking your knowledge away and making these new interests into reinforcers. E.g. If you see your child hiding under a blanket, maybe their reinforcer could be making a den. This one would need a token system to build up to the main reward.

"We have a big family, our 5-year-old son is autistic and he is one of 4 boys. We also have a daughter who is 11. Our children are the perfect ages for a Disneyland holiday but we are so worried that our autistic child won't be able to cope being there. He gets overstimulated quite easily and the things we use to help him calm down are impractical to take along with us. For example his miniature trampoline.

My husband and I have even talked about splitting the family for the Disney trip but we just can't bring ourselves to do it. What is your advice to us for our situation?"

I would say go ahead with the trip! But make sure you take the time to prepare your son with autism. I understand that some of his sensory regulators may not be appropriate to take with you, what I'd say is look at what type of feedback your son it getting from his trampoline. For example; would he gain the same feedback from jumping on bubble wrap?

Here are some ideas that may make your trip a little easier on your son:

- ✔ Take a small sensory bag with you when you're out and about. Fill it with items that will help calm your son if he is feeling overstimulated. (See *'Sensory Integration, Part Five'*, page 65 for a full list of items.)

✔ Take an MP3 or Apple device so that your child can block the noise out at Disney if necessary with calming music.

✔ Prepare your son with a sensory story breaking down the parts of your trip, add as much detail as possible with pictures. Read the story each day for at least a week before you go away and don't forget to take the story with you.

✔ Show your son pictures of Disney online and show him parts of the park you will visit on the map

✔ Finally, take some home comforts along with you, for example, your son's breakfast bowl, pillow for bedtime or drinking cup.

"At home, we are working on teaching our daughter about emotions. She knows happy and sad but doesn't necessarily always use them in the correct context. She really struggles recognising different emotions and also relating to people's emotions. For example, if her friend was to fall over and hurt herself she wouldn't check if she was okay. We also had her Grandfather staying with us for a month not long ago and she really enjoying being with him but when it was time for him to leave she was reluctant to even say goodbye. She showed no emotion at all. What can I do to help her?"

Many children on the spectrum struggle with understanding emotions and empathy. Often it's something that does not come naturally to children with autism like it does to neuro-typical people. Which means parents and carers need to work hard to teach emotions.

There are many ways of doing this, but use the strategy most suited to your daughter's ability. Here are a few great ideas to get you started...

• Take photos of yourself and other close family members or friends (people that your daughter is familiar with)

displaying different emotions. Use the cards to teach her these emotions.

Try not to focus on just happy and sad. There are loads of emotions out there that you can teach. Try, excited, surprised, confused, unwell, frustrated. Once a few are taught, try playing cards in pairs, for a fun way to solidify her knowledge.

- Make an effort to tell your daughter how you are feeling when you are displaying emotion.

For example, if driving and you're frustrated because you're in traffic. You could turn to her and say "I'm so frustrated with all of this traffic we are in."

- Over exaggerate your facial expressions and ask her to copy you.

Yes, you probably will look silly, but if your expression is not clear this may confuse your daughter even more. Use a mirror as it often helps when children can see their own face when they do this. When you first ask her to copy you, take it slow and if she struggles do not worry too much. Initially, the main thing is that she is being exposed to different emotions.

Empathy is a harder one to teach as I find it's easier to teach in a more natural environment as and when the situation arises. Take your daughter aside and talk with her about possible things she could say to her friend if they were hurt. Role play is also a lovely way of practising these skills.

A Special gift from *'The Ambitious Autism Ambassador'*

Before you go any further, make sure you go to www.unlimitedautismsuccess.com/book-resources and claim over £47 worth of additional tools and templates to help you get the very best from your child with autism.

Here's just some of what you'll get:

- Templates and ideas to help you better manage your child's behaviour

- Additional resources to help aid and improve your child's communication

- Helpful hints and tips to make sure your child is getting the support they need at school

- A ton of things you and the family can do to help your child progress socially and form bonds with others.

- And much more...

To get your FREE bonuses go to...
www.unlimitedautismsuccess.com/book-resources *now.*

Conclusion

If there's one thing I want you to take away from this book, then it's this...

*The proven strategies and information I've shared with you will **ONLY** work if you put them into practice.*

You can read all the best tips that will help you understand your autistic child better, but if you don't implement anything, all that reading is pointless.

But I believe in you.

I believe that with one baby step at a time, every parent and carer can discover a deep understanding of their child's needs. And they can discover how to form a close, meaningful bond with their child, all the while helping them learn new skills. You just need to stick with it. On the up days, stay positive and share your child's achievements with their school and with your family to keep the ball rolling. And on the down days, pick up this book flick through some of the Q&A's to help you out, remember you're not on your own, and remember to take a deep breath before you deal with anything.

Never blame yourself, focus on the positives and the only way is up!

I honestly believe that you can spend as much or as little money as you want, but if you don't put in the work and time, your child will not progress.

So...

Be committed to doing all you can to help your autistic child thrive, be willing to invest time into YOUR CHILD'S development by implementing the proven strategies in this book to help your child reach their full potential.

About Me

I'm Emma Ottaway, The Ambitious Autism Ambassador....I started working with autistic children whilst I was at college. I quickly took a keen interest in Autism and found myself 'taking my work home with me' like, reading up on Autism and continuously thinking of different methods I could use to help the children I was working with. After working in my first Special Needs School, it was clear to me that this was the career path for me.

For well over half a decade now I've been working in mainstream and special schools, ASD units and SEN departments, I have also worked closely supporting children with learning difficulties, mentoring vulnerable teenagers and managing challenging behaviours within schools and at home.

I strongly believe every child should have a positive role model supporting them in their lives and ensuring that they receive the opportunities in which they deserve to reach their goals and dreams.

I have a real passion and drive for supporting autistic children in reaching their full potential and overcoming any personal challenges they may be facing in their lives.

My vision is to help parents in need of support with their autistic children, to teach parents how to really get the best out of their children, build their relationship with them and to manage and understand their children's behaviours to create a happy and fulfilled family life.

Acknowledgments

Thank you to every single child I've had the pleasure of working with, for intriguing me, inspiring me and truly captivating me.

Thank you for trusting me and holding onto my hand as you ventured out of your silent world into my loud, confusing one. You've taught me everything I know!

I'd also like to thank my partner Drew, my best friend. I couldn't have got here without your constant support and love. Sometimes it was tough love, but you were right all along! Thank you for every word of encouragement you gave along my journey. Your work ethic inspires me everyday.

Lightning Source UK Ltd.
Milton Keynes UK
UKOW05f0319191116
288008UK00002B/24/P